Phrase**Guide**

GW00567357

GREEK

With menu decoder, survival guide and two-way dictionary

Thomas Cook Publishing

www.thomascookpublishing.com

Survival guide...................49

Emergencies.....................59

Dictionary........................63

Quick reference..............95

How to use this guide
The ten chapters in this guide are colour-coded to help you find what you're looking for. These colours are used on the tabs of the pages and in the contents on the opposite page and above.

For quick reference, you'll find some basic expressions on the inside front cover and essential emergency phrases on the inside back cover. There is also a handy reference section for numbers, measurements and clothes sizes at the back of the guide.

Front cover photography © Jacob Halaska/www.photolibrary.com
Cover design/artwork by Sharon Edwards
Photos: Chrissi Nerantzi (p5) and Markus Biehal (p33)

Produced by The Content Works Ltd
www.thecontentworks.com
Design concept: Mike Wade
Layout: Tika Stefano & Pat Hinsley
Text: Amanda Castleman
Editing: Marianna Toliou & Amanda Castleman
Proofing: Wendy Janes
Project editor: Begoña Juarros
Management: Lisa Plumridge & Rik Mulder

Published by Thomas Cook Publishing
A division of Thomas Cook Tour Operations Limited
PO Box 227, Unit 18, Coningsby Road
Peterborough PE3 8SB, United Kingdom
Company Registration No 1450464 England
email: books@thomascook.com
www.thomascookpublishing.com
+44 (0)1733 416477

ISBN-13: 978-1-84157-672-5

First edition © 2007 Thomas Cook Publishing
Text © 2007 Thomas Cook Publishing

Project Editor: Kelly Pipes
Production/DTP: Steven Collins

Printed and bound in Italy by Printer Trento

Introduction

Greek is the language of mythology, philosophy and epic poetry. Many of the bedrock classics of Western civilisation sprang from this Mediterranean nation. Its ancient culture infuses our modern one – from democracy to the Oedipus complex.

Most travellers associate the tongue more with sun-soaked package holidays, "following the herd down to Greece," as Blur sang in 1994's *Girls and Boys*. Among the island hopping and ouzo, take time to explore a few ruins – and make some foreign friends with the help of this phrasebook.

The basics

The Greek language influenced ours greatly. Nonetheless, most foreigners struggle with the unfamiliar alphabet and sounds. Push beyond the fear factor, because in remote areas you'll be speaking the native tongue more often than English. And even in tourist hotspots, a little Greek goes a long way towards establishing goodwill.

Around 13 million people speak this language worldwide, mostly centred in Greece and Cyprus. It evolved from ancient Greek – spoken by Homer, Plato, Socrates and Sappho – and traces back to Indo-European.

Its oldest writing style, called Linear B, dates from the 14th to 12th centuries BC. The Greeks adapted Phoenician letters, becoming the first to feature vowels, by the 9th century. Four hundred years later, the script gave birth to the Latin alphabet (used for English and other western European languages) and Cyrillic (used in Slavic languages).

The spoken language varied wildly, depending on the scope of the empire, invasions and pop culture. For example, Alexander the Great conquered people far into Persia, spreading the Attic dialect (spoken in Attica – the province around Athens – not found among the rafters). This Eastern Roman Empire and Orthodox Church spoke this way for centuries.

The Ottomans captured Constantinople (now Istanbul) in 1453, forcing Attic Greek underground. The people kept speaking the common tongue, dubbed **koine**, however. A rich canon of songs emerged – spiced by Turkish, Italian, Albanian and other Balkan words.

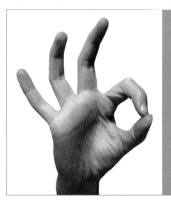

False friends

To say "no," Greeks once nodded their heads upward and raised their eyebrows – which smacks of "yes" elsewhere. Similarly, the "OK" gesture (thumb to index finger) is an insult here traditionally.

In 1821, Greece rebelled and created a new country. A debate waged over its official language: posh **katharevousa** versus humble **dimotiki**, which means 'popular'. The simpler, more widespread tongue was the choice and persists today (though briefly deposed during the military junta of 1967-74).

English owes Greek – in its many forms – a huge debt. Many of our more grandiose concepts draw from its vocabulary: astronomy, cosmos, democracy, drama, ideas, mathematics, mythology, politics, and so forth. The language also gave us aeroplanes, biology, electricity, photography, psychology, technology and telephones ... even the word 'alphabet' itself.

The shared terms don't help visitors much, unless they're holding forth on Pluto's demotion or the West End's latest offerings. Instead, it's best to learn simple phrases.

Grammar

Don't let the alphabet intimidate you too much. For example, Greek has a large number of diphthongs: two vowels sandwiched together. Most boil down to a simple sound (go with 'e' if one is present).

Review these consonant combinations – and if all else fails, remember that **bar** is 'bar':

μπ – 'b' at the beginning, as in *b*ird; 'mb' in the middle, as in ba*mb*oo

ντ – 'd' at the beginning, as in *d*emand; 'nd' in the middle, as in da*nd*elion

γκ – 'g' at the beginning, as in *g*oal; 'ng' in the middle, as in a*ng*uish

γγ – 'ng' as in a*ng*le

τσ – 'ts' as in ca*ts*

τζ – 'tz' as in *tz*atziki

Watch for the accent marks, which indicate where you should stress the word.

There are three genders in Greek: masculine, feminine and neuter. Nouns are listed with their article: **o** for masculine, **η** for feminine, **το** for neuter and **οι** (both masculine and feminine) **ή τα** (neuter) for plural. For example: **δρόμος, o** (road), **διαδρομή, η** (route), **στάδιο, το** (stadium). If nouns can be either masculine or feminine, they are displayed as: **γιατρός, ο/η** (doctor). Adjectives agree with nouns in gender, case and number and are placed in front of the noun. We display adjectives in the following format: **ωραίος/α/ο**; *oreos/a/o m/f/n* (nice). For example, **ωραίος δρόμος**; *oreos dhromos* – nice road, **ωραία διαδρομή**; *orea dhiadromi* – nice route, **ωραίο στάδιο**; *oreo stadhio* – nice stadium.

Greek isn't the easiest language – you can't fake this from childhood Latin or French – but it's among the most rewarding. Master a few phrases and doors fly open; locals truly appreciate the effort.

Basic conversation

Hello	**Γεια σας**	*ya sas*
Goodbye	**Αντίο**	*andeeo*
Yes	**Ναι**	*ne*
No	**Όχι**	*okhee*
Please	**Παρακαλώ**	*parakalo*
Thank you	**Ευχαριστώ**	*efkhareesto*
You're welcome	**Παρακαλώ**	*parakalo*
Sorry	**Συγγνώμη**	*sighnomi*
Excuse me (apology)	**Με συγχωρείτε**	*me singkhorite*
Excuse me (to get attention)	**Συγγνώμη**	*sighnomi*
Excuse me (to get past)	**Συγγνώμη**	*sighnomi*
Do you speak English?	**Μιλάτε αγγλικά;**	*milate angglika?*
I don't speak Greek	**Δεν μιλώ ελληνικά**	*then milo elinika*
I speak a little Greek	**Μιλώ λίγα ελληνικά**	*milo ligha elinika*
What?	**Συγγνώμη;**	*sighnomi?*
I understand	**Καταλαβαίνω**	*katalaveno*
I don't understand	**Δεν καταλαβαίνω**	*dhen katalaveno*
Do you understand?	**Καταλαβαίνετε;**	*katalavenete?*
I don't know	**Δεν ξέρω**	*dhen ksero*
I can't	**Δεν μπορώ**	*then boro*
Can you... please?	**Θα μπορούσατε ...;**	*tha borusate...?*
- speak more slowly	**- να μιλάτε λίγο πιο αργά;**	*- na milate ligho pio argha?*
- repeat that	**- να το επαναλάβετε;**	*- na to epanalavete?*

Greetings

Outside tourist hotspots, locals are more inquisitive and friendly. The warm welcome traces back to the ancient Greeks, who believed in **xenophilia** – a host's sacred obligation to feed and protect strangers.

Titles remain important here: greet authorities, strangers and older folk with **Kirie** (Mr) or **Kiria** (Mrs/Ms). Always use the formal, polite forms – like **esis** rather than **esi** for 'you' – until invited to be more intimate and casual.

Cheek kisses are common among friends, but a nod and handshake suffice for new business acquaintances.

Meeting someone

Hello	Γεια σας	*ya sas*
Hi	Γεια	*ya*
Good morning	Καλημέρα	*kaleem_e_ra*
Good afternoon	Καλησπέρα	*kaleesp_e_ra*
Good evening	Καληνύχτα	*kaleen_ee_khta*
Sir/Mr	Κύριε	*kirie*
Madam/Mrs	Κυρία	*kiria*
Miss	Δεσποινίς	*thesp_i_nis*
How are you?	Πώς είστε;	*pos _ee_ste?*
Fine, thank you	Καλά, ευχαριστώ	*kala, efkhareest_o_*
And you?	Εσείς;	*es_ee_s?*
Very well	Πολύ καλά	*pol_ee_ kala*
Not very well	Όχι και πολύ καλά	*_o_khi ke pol_ee_ kala*

Third degree

Greeks enjoy topics off-limits in British small talk, such as income, home price, age, illness and cures for your excess blubber. Don't be offended by this forthright culture.

Small talk

My name is...	Με λένε...	*me l_e_ne...*
What's your name?	Πώς σας λένε;	*pos sas l_e_ne?*
I'm pleased to meet you	Χαίρω πολύ για τη γνωριμία	*_h_ero pol_ee_ yia tee ghnoreem_ee_a*
Where are you from?	Από πού είστε;	*_a_po pu _ee_ste?*
I am from Britain	Είμαι από την Αγγλία	*_ee_me _a_po teen angg_li_a*

Do you live here?	Μένετε εδώ;	*menete etho?*
This is a great...	Αυτή είναι μια απίθανη...	*afti ine mia apeethanee...*
- country	- χώρα	*- khora*
- city/town	- πόλη	*- poli*
I am staying at...	Μένω στο...	*meno sto...*

I'm here for...	Θα είμαι εδώ για...	*tha eeme etho yia...*
- the day	- μία ημέρα	*- mia imera*
- a weekend	- το Σαββατοκύριακο	*- to savatokiriako*
- a week	- μία εβδομάδα	*- mia evthomatha*

| How old are you? | Πόσο χρονών είστε; | *poso khronon iste?* |
| I'm... years old | Είμαι... χρονών | *ime... khronon* |

Family

This is my...	Από εδώ...	*apo etho...*
- husband	- ο σύζυγός μου	*- o sizighos mu*
- wife	- η σύζυγός μου	*- ee sizighos mu*
- friend	- ο φίλος μου *m/* η φίλη μου *f*	*- o filos mu/ ee fili mu*
- boyfriend/ girlfriend	- το αγόρι μου/ η κοπέλα μου	*- to aghori mu/ ee kopela mu*

I have a...	Έχω...	*ekho...*
- son	- ένα γιο	*- ena yio*
- daughter	- μία κόρη	*- mia kori*
- grandson	- έναν εγγονό	*- enan egono*
- granddaughter	- μία εγγονή	*- mia egoni*

Do you have...	Έχετε...	*ekhete...*
- children?	- παιδιά;	*- pethia?*
- grandchildren?	- εγγόνια;	*- egonia?*
I don't have children	Δεν έχω παιδιά	*then ekho pethia*

| Are you married? | Είστε παντρεμένος; *m/* Είστε παντρεμένη; *f* | *eeste padremenos?/ eeste padremeni?* |

I'm...	Είμαι...	*eeme...*
- single	- ανύπαντρος *m/* ανύπαντρη *f*	*- anipadros/ anipadri*
- married	- παντρεμένος *m/* παντρεμένη *f*	*- padremenos/ padremeni*

11

| - divorced | - χωρισμένος m/ χωρισμένη f | - khorizmenos/ khorizmeni |
| - widowed | - χήρος m/χήρα f | - khiros/khira |

Saying goodbye

Goodbye	Αντίο	adheeo
Good night	Καληνύχτα	kaleeneekhta
Sleep well	Όνειρα γλυκά	oneera ghleeka
See you later	Τα λέμε	ta leme
Have a good trip	Καλό ταξίδι	kalo taksithi
It was nice meeting you	Χάρηκα για τη γνωριμία	harika yia tee ghnoreemeea
Have fun	Καλά να περάσετε	kala na perasete
Good luck	Καλή τύχη	kalee teehi
Keep in touch	Μη χαθούμε	mi khathume
My address is...	Η διεύθυνσή μου είναι...	i thiefthinsi mu ine...
What's your...	Ποια είναι... (f)/ Ποιο είναι... (n)	pia ine.../ pio ine...
- address?	- η διεύθυνσή σας; f	- i thiefthinsi sas?
- email?	- το email σας; n	- to imeil sas?
- telephone number?	- το τηλέφωνό σας; n	- to tilefono sas?

Bearing gifts

Famed for their hospitality, Greeks pull out all the stops for guests. Show appreciation with a small gift, perhaps a beautifully wrapped bouquet, cake or box of chocolates.

Eating out

Eating is an event, a leisure activity, even a lifestyle here. Don't expect brisk service. Breakfast is normally hot tea or coffee with toast or **tiropita**, a cheese pastry. Lunch is the main meal, sprawling through the afternoon whenever possible. Dinner is lighter and served between 8 and 9pm. Most Greeks prefer fresh fruit for dessert.

In rural areas, many cafés and restaurants don't accept credit cards, so carry cash. Restaurant bills may include a 15 per cent service charge. Additional tipping is not required, but leave up to 10 per cent for great service.

Introduction

Much of the country's social life centres around cuisine. Anyone in a rush should simply grab a sandwich or **tiropita**. Restaurants are for lingering. The café culture also encourages languid people-watching. These establishments shade from coffee to cocktails as the day progresses, and may serve light snacks. Children are welcome in all but the tiniest lounges.

I'd like...	Θα ήθελα...	tha _ithela..._
- a table for (two)	- ένα τραπέζι για (δύο) άτομα	- _ena trapezi yia (thio) atoma_
- a sandwich	- ένα σάντουιτς	- _ena sanduits_
- a coffee	- ένα καφέ	- _ena kafe_
- a tea (with milk)	- ένα τσάι (με γάλα)	- _ena tsai (me ghala)_
Do you have a menu in English?	Έχετε ένα μενού στα αγγλικά;	_ekhete ena menu sta angglika?_
The bill, please	Το λογαριασμό, παρακαλώ	_to loghariazmo, parakalo_

You may hear...

στους καπνίζοντες/ στους μη καπνίζοντες;	_stus kapnizodes/stus mi kapnizodes?_	Smoking or non-smoking?
Τι θα θέλατε;	_ti tha thelate?_	What are you going to have?

The cuisines of Greece

National specialities

Greeks prefer an array of simple dishes, often just meat or vegetables braised with **elaiolado** (olive oil) and **lemoni** (lemon). Roast lamb, garnished with rosemary, is a tradition here, as is garlic-infused yoghurt. Basil is popular as decoration and for good luck, but rarely appears in dishes. Oregano is more the herb of choice.

Signature dishes

(see the Menu decoder for more dishes)

Τζατζίκι	_tzatzeekee_	Garlic, cucumber and yoghurt dip
Γύρος	_yeeros_	Doner kebab
Χωριάτικη σαλάτα	_khoriatiki salata_	Classic 'village' salad: tomatoes, cucumber olives, feta cheese

| Αρνάκι ψητό | *arn<u>a</u>ki ps<u>ee</u>to* | Roast lamb |
| Μπακλαβάς | *baklav<u>as</u>* | Filo pastry with honey and nuts |

Posh plates in Athens

Kolonaki, Athens' see-and-be-seen district, is filled with trendy eateries. Celebrate special occasions further up the hill at elegant Orizontes Lykavyttou (reservations essential; on top of Lycabettus hill; 210 722 7065).

Peloponnese

Coastal delicacies include octopus baked in paper – hence the sea creatures draped out to dry. Inland, cooks deftly use the fruits of the orchard, like apples, figs, raisins and honey. The western peninsula is known for its wines, including **nemeas** and **achaia klaous**.

Signature dishes

(see the Menu decoder for more dishes)

Γουρουνόπουλο	*gooroo<u>o</u>nopoolo*	Herb-roasted sucking pig
Ελιές καλαμών	*el<u>ye</u>s kal<u>a</u>mon*	Kalamata olives
Τουρλού	*toorl<u>oo</u>*	Ratatouille
Δίπλες	*dh<u>ee</u>ples*	Honey-walnut pastry
Μηλόπιτα	*mil<u>o</u>pita*	Apple pie with cinnamon

The Ionian Islands

Italian flavours spice this western archipelago, washed by the Ionian Sea. Fresh fish and game are both popular, sometimes paired with garlic sauce from nearby Corfu. The barley rusks of Lefkada are delicacies, as well as polenta dishes.

Signature dishes
(see the Menu decoder for more dishes)

Πίτες	*peetes*	Savoury pies
Φασολάδα	*fasolatha*	Thick vegetable and haricot bean soup
Γίδα βραστή	*yeetha vrastee*	Goat meat soup with lemon
Κυνήγι	*keeniyi*	Game
Μπουγάτσα	*boogatsa*	Vanilla custard pie with cinnamon

Dig in, but don't ante in Greeks typically share **mezedes**, as well as main courses and desserts. Eating is a communal affair. However, the bill is not. Whoever issued the invitation typically pays the cheque.

Crete
The rugged southern island is famed for its olives, olive oils and **chorta** (wild greens). The seafood is outstanding, as might be expected. Wash it all down with **kritikos**, the local wine.

Signature dishes
(see the Menu decoder for more dishes)

Γραβιέρα	*gravee-era*	Graviera cheese, similar to gruyère
Σύκα	*seeka*	Figs
Σαλιγκάρια	*saleengareea*	Snails
Χοιρινό κρητικό	*heereeno kriteeko*	Pork chops with spicy vegetable sauce
Καρπούζι	*karpoozee*	Watermelon

Taste of Atlantis?

Santorini is the star of the Cycladic Islands: a crescent rind left around an ocean-filled volcanic crater, rumoured to be Atlantis. The local delicacy is **fava**, beans cooked to mush, served cold with lemon.

Aegean Islands

Sprawling towards Turkey, these eastern islands play with Ottoman flavours: cardamom, sesame, yoghurt and currants. Squid, crab and oysters all feature here, as well as an extensive array of cheese. Exceptional wines echo the names of the islands: Samos, Santorini and Paros.

Signature dishes

(see the Menu decoder for more dishes)

Φάβα	_fava_	Beans cooked to mush, served cold with lemon
Κακαβιά	kakavee_a_	Fish soup
Μυδοπίλαφο	meedo_pee_lafo	Seafood pilaf
Παστίτσιο	pas_tee_tsyo	Macaroni and mince pie
Χταπόδι κρασάτο	khta_po_thee kra_sa_to	Octopus in white wine

Thrace & Macedonia

Immigrants from the Turkish coast brought spice to this northern region: saffron and chilli, mint and paprika. Meat features more in stews, less as great haunches here. The Mount Athos monks' wines are especially renowned.

Signature dishes
(see the Menu decoder for more dishes)

Ντολμάδες	*dolmadhes*	Rice-stuffed vine leaves
Τουρσί	*toorsee*	Pickled vegetables
Τυροκαυτερή	*teerokafteree*	Feta and red pepper dip
Τας κεμπάμπ	*tash kebab*	Grilled meat in spicy sauce
Κανταΐφι	*kanda-eefee*	Filo pastry with honey and nuts

Wine, beer & spirits

Ouzo is the country's most famous drink. The aniseed spirit turns cloudy when mixed with ice or water. Unless buying a posh bottle, order wine by the carafe – **karafa krasi**. The copper beakers come in several sizes. Greece's beers are undistinguished; Mythos is a popular brand, but the Danish Ceres remains more popular.

Ούζο	*uzo*	Aniseed-flavoured spirit
Μεταξά	*metakhsa*	Greek brandy
Τσίπουρο	*tsipuro*	High-alcohol grape spirit
Ρετσίνα	*retsina*	Pine-seasoned white wine
Κουμανταρία	*kumandaria*	Cypriot wine

Passable red from Patras
The country's third largest city is home to Achaia Clauss winery. Franz Liszt, Aristotle Onassis and Margaret Thatcher all visited the 'imperial cellar', home to 128 rare barrels worth millions of euros.

No bottoms up
Draining your wine glass is gauche. A considerate host refills smoothly, long before you hit the bottom. Light drinkers should mix in water – or leave the glass over half full to show they're done.

Could I have...	Θα ήθελα...	*tha ithela...*
- a beer?	- μία μπύρα;	- *mea bira?*
- a glass/a bottle of white/red/rosé wine?	- ένα ποτήρι/μπουκάλι άσπρο/κόκκινο/ροζέ κρασί;	- *ena potiri/bukali aspro/kokino/ roze krasee?*
- a glass/a bottle of champagne?	- ένα ποτήρι/μπουκάλι σαμπάνια;	- *ena potiri/bukali sampania?*

You may hear...

Τι θα πάρετε;	*ti tha parete?*	What can I get you?
Πώς θα το πάρετε;	*pos tha to parete?*	How would you like it?
Με ή χωρίς πάγο;	*me i khoris pagho?*	With or without ice?
Κρύο ή θερμοκρασία δωματίου;	*krio ee thermokrasia thomatioo?*	Cold or room temperature?

Snacks & refreshments

Greek coffee is fierce and strong, thick with grounds at the cup's bottom. Ask for your **ellinikos kafes** with milk (**me gala**) or without (**choris gala**). The country has a good selection of fast food – usually sandwiches or savoury pastries – but supermarkets still have restricted hours. News kiosks selling drinks and snacks never close in cities, however.

Γιαούρτι	*yaoortee*	Yoghurt
Γύρος	*yeeros*	Doner kebab
Καφές	*kafes*	Coffee

| Ούζο | _uzo_ | Ouzo: aniseed-flavoured spirit |
| Σπανακόπιτα | spana_ko_peeta | Spinach pie |

Vegetarians & special requirements

I'm vegetarian	Είμαι χορτοφάγος _m/f_	_ime khortofaghos_
I don't eat...	Δεν τρώω...	_then tro-o..._
- meat	- κρέας	- _kreas_
- fish	- ψάρι	- _psari_

Could you cook something without meat in it?	Μπορείτε να μαγειρέψετε κάτι χωρίς κρέας;	_borite na mayirepsete kati khoris kreas?_
What's in this?	Με τι είναι φτιαγμένο αυτό;	_me tee ine fteea-ghmeno afto?_
I'm allergic to...	Είμαι αλλεργικός/ αλλεργική _(m/f)_ σε...	_ime aleryikos/ aleryiki se..._
- nuts	- ξηρούς καρπούς	- _ksirus karpus_
- wheat	- προϊόντα σιταριού	- _proeeonda sitariu_
- dairy	- γαλακτομικά προϊόντα	- _ghalaktomika proeeonda_

Children

Are children welcome?	Επιτρέπονται τα παιδιά;	_epitreponte ta pethia?_
Do you have a children's menu?	Έχετε ένα παιδικό μενού;	_ekhete ena pethiko menu?_
What dishes are good for children?	Ποια πιάτα είναι καλά για τα παιδιά;	_pia piata ine kala ya ta pethia?_

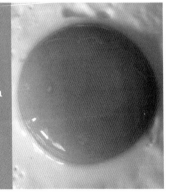

Holiday like Shirley Valentine

One day, her stodgy husband sneered at his egg and chips. So the middle-aged Liverpudlian housewife gallivanted off to Greece. Lewis Gilbert's 1989 film, *Shirley Valentine*, inspired countless holidays.

Menu decoder

Essentials

Breakfast	Πρωϊνό	*proeeno*
Lunch	Μεσημεριανό	*mesimeriano*
Dinner	Δείπνο	*thipno*
Cover charge	Κουβέρ	*koover*
VAT inclusive	Το ΦΠΑ συμπεριλαμβάνεται	*to fi pi a simberilamvanete*
Service included	Το σέρβις συμπεριλαμβάνεται	*to service simberi-lamvanete*
Credit cards (not) accepted	(Δεν) Δεχόμαστε πιστωτικές κάρτες	*(then) thekhomaste pistotikes kartes*
First course	Πρώτο πιάτο/Ορεκτικά	*proto piato/orektika*
Second course	Κύριο πιάτο	*kirio piato*
Dessert	Επιδόρπιο	*epithorpio*
Dish of the day	Πιάτο της ημέρας	*pyato tees imeras*
Local speciality	Τοπική σπεσιαλιτέ	*topiki specialite*
Set menu	Υποχρεωτικό μενού/ταμπλ ντ'οτ	*eepochreoteeko menu/tabl dot*
A la carte menu	Μενού α λα καρτ	*menu a la kart*
Tourist menu	Τουριστικό μενού	*tooristiko menu*
Wine list	Μενού κρασιών	*menu krasyon*
Drinks menu	Μενού ποτών	*menu poton*
Snack menu	Μενού μεζέδων	*menu mezedon*

Opa!

Smashing glasses isn't very common anymore. Some music joints – featuring **laika** (bouzouki ballads) or **rembetika** (Greek blues) – still permit showers of shards. However, you'll pay dearly for the dramatic moment.

Halloumi cheese

Now a Cypriot speciality, Halloumi was first produced by Middle Eastern Bedouins. Made from ewe's and sometimes goat's milk, it's kneaded with chopped mint during manufacture and served grilled or fried.

Methods of preparation

Baked	Στο φούρνο	*sto foorno*
Boiled	Βρασμένο	*vrazmeno*
Braised	Ψημένο στη σχάρα	*psimeno sti skhara*
Breaded	Παναρισμένο	*panarismeno*
Deep-fried	Τηγανισμένο σε καυτό λάδι	*tighanizmeno se kafto ladhi*
Fresh	Φρέσκο	*fresko*
Fried	Τηγανητό	*tighanito*
Frozen	Κατεψυγμένο	*katepsighmeno*
Grilled/broiled	Στα κάρβουνα	*sta karvuna*
Marinated	Μαριναρισμένο	*marinarismeno*
Mashed	Πουρές	*pures*
Poached	Βρασμένο	*vrazmeno*
Raw	Ωμό	*omo*
Roasted	Ψητό	*pseeto*
Salty	Αλμυρό	*almiro*
Sautéed	Σοτέ	*sote*
Smoked	Καπνιστό	*kapneesto*
Spicy (flavour)	Πικάντικο	*pikandiko*
Spicy (hot)	Πιπεράτο	*piperato*
Steamed	Βρασμένο στον ατμό	*vrazmeno ston atmo*

Stewed	Μαγειρευτό	*mayeerefto*
Stuffed	Γεμιστό	*yemisto*
Sweet	Γλυκό	*ghleeko*
Rare	Σενιάν	*senian*
Medium	Ψημένο κανονικά	*psimeno kanonika*
Well done	Καλοψημένο	*kalopsimeno*

Common food items

Beef	Βοδινό	*vodheeno*
Chicken	Κοτόπουλο	*kotopoolo*
Turkey	Γαλοπούλα	*ghalapoola*
Lamb	Αρνάκι	*arnee*
Pork	Χοιρινό	*kheereeno*
Fish	Ψάρι	*psari*
Seafood	Θαλασσινά	*thalaseena*
Tuna	Τόνος	*tonos*
Beans	Φασόλια	*fasolia*
Cheese	Τυρί	*teeree*
Eggs	Αυγά	*avgha*
Lentils	Φακές	*fakes*
Pasta/noodles	Ζυμαρικά	*zeemarika*
Rice	Ρύζι	*reezi*
Aubergine	Μελιτζάνα	*meleetzana*
Cabbage	Λάχανο	*lakhano*
Carrot	Καρότο	*karoto*
Cucumber	Αγγούρι	*angooree*
Garlic	Σκόρδο	*skordho*
Mushrooms	Μανιτάρια	*maneetareea*

Taramosalata

Originally made from salted and cured carps' roe, the version you're more likely to find today will be cod roe mixed with lemon juice, onions, garlic and olive oil. Enjoy it with crudités or warm pita bread.

Olives	Ελιές	*elyes*
Onion	Κρεμμύδι	*kremmithi*
Potato	Πατάτες	*patates*
Red/green pepper	Κόκκινη/πράσινη πιπεριά	*kokeenee/praseenee piperia*
Tomato	Ντομάτα	*dhomata*
Vegetables	Λαχανικά	*lakhanika*

Bread	Ψωμί	*psomee*
Oil	Λάδι	*ladhee*
Pepper	Πιπέρι	*peeperi*
Salt	Αλάτι	*alati*
Vinegar	Ξύδι	*kseedhee*
Cake	Κέικ	*cake*
Cereal	Δημητριακά	*dimitriaka*
Cream	Κρέμα	*krema*
Fruit	Φρούτα	*froota*
Ice cream	Παγωτό	*paghoto*
Milk	Γάλα	*ghala*
Tart	Τάρτα	*tarta*

Kalamata olives
In the Gulf of Messinia, Kalamata is known the world over for its aubergine-coloured, rich and fruity olives and olive oil.

Popular sauces

Ελαιόλαδο	*eleoladho*	Olive oil
Λαδολέμονο	*latholemono*	Olive oil and lemon
Λαδόξυδο	*lathoksitho*	Oil and vinegar
Λεμόνι	*lemoni*	Lemon
Μελιτζανοσαλάτα	*meleetzana salata*	Aubergine dip
Κέτσαπ	*ketsap*	Ketchup
Σάλτσα πιπεριάς	*saltsa piperias*	Chilli sauce
Ταραμοσαλάτα	*taramosalata*	Cod roe dip
Ταχίνι	*tahini*	Sesame seed paste

| Τζατζίκι | *tzat<u>zee</u>kee* | Garlic, cucumber and yoghurt dip |
| Χούμους | *<u>khoo</u>mous* | Hummus (chick-peas, sesame) |

Greek tapas

Make a meal of **mezedes** (tasting dishes) washed down with ouzo. Order off the menu or simply point as waiters circulate trays of garlic potato mash, marinated peppers, pickled octopus and Kalamata olives.

Starters & mezedes

Αυγολέμονο σούπα	*avgho<u>le</u>mono <u>su</u>pa*	Egg and lemon soup
Γαΐδουρελιά	*ghaithure<u>lia</u>*	Large 'donkey' olives
Γίγαντες	*<u>yee</u>ghantes*	Large butter beans in tomato sauce
Δίπλες Δράμας	*<u>thi</u>ples <u>thra</u>mas*	Yogurt pie with vine leaves
Ελαιόπιτες	*eleopites*	Cypriot olive and leek pie
Καλαμάρι τηγανητό	*kala<u>ma</u>ri tighani<u>to</u>*	Battered squid rings or strips
Λουκάνικα	*loo<u>ka</u>neeka*	Seasoned sausage
Ντολμάδες	*dol<u>ma</u>dhes*	Rice-stuffed vine leaves
Σκορδαλιά	*skordhhal<u>ya</u>*	Garlic and potato mash
Σούπα φακές ξιδάτη	*<u>su</u>pa fa<u>kes</u> ksi<u>ta</u>ti*	Sour lentil soup
Φασόλια σαλάτα	*fa<u>so</u>lia sa<u>la</u>ta*	Bean salad
Χαλούμι	*kha<u>loo</u>mee*	Halloumi: rubbery ewe's cheese, usually grilled
Χωριάτικη σαλάτα	*khori<u>a</u>tiki sa<u>la</u>ta*	Classic 'village' salad: tomatoes, cucumber, olives, feta cheese

Second course dishes

Αγριογούρουνο	agreeogooroono	Wild boar
Αρνάκι ψητό	arnaki pseeto	Roast lamb
Γαλοπούλα γεμιστή	ghalopula yemisti	Stuffed roast turkey
Γαρίδες σαγανάκι	gharithes saghanaki	Fried prawns with tomatoes, red wine, baked feta
Γεμιστά	yemeesta	Stuffed vegetables
Καλαμάρια τηγανητά	kalamareea teeghaneeta	Fried squid
Μακαρόνια	makaronya	Macaroni
Μελανούρι	melanuri	Sea bream
Μουσακάς	musakas	Baked aubergine and mince
Μύδια	mithia	Mussels
Ουρά βοδιού	ura vothiu	Oxtail
Ραβιόλια	raviolia	Cheese and mint ravioli
Χταπόδι κεφτέδες	khtapothee keftethes	Rissoles of octopus, onion, mint and cheese
Χταπόδι στιφάδο	khtapothee stifatho	Octopus ragout

Side dishes

Αγγουροσαλάτα	anggurosalata	Sliced, salted cucumber
Βρούβες	vruves	Peppery field greens
Ιμάμ μπαϊλντί	eemam baeeldee	Stuffed aubergines
Κεφαλοτύρι (τηγανητό ή ψητό)	kefaloteeree (teeghaneeto ee pseeto)	Cheese, usually fried in olive oil or grilled
Κεφτέδες	keftedhes	Meatballs
Μελιτζάνες ιμάμ	meleetzanes eemam	Aubergine stuffed with tomato, onion
Ντομάτες γεμιστές	domates yemeestes	Stuffed tomatoes
Πατάτες ριγανάτες στο φούρνο	patates righanates sto furno	Roasted potatoes with oregano
Πιλάφι	peelafee	Rice
Πίτα	peeta	Flat, unleavened bread
Χόρτα	khorta	Wild greens with olive oil and lemon
Χορτοσαλάτα	khortosalata	Warm green salad with lemon
Χυλοπίτες	hilopites	Hot macaroni with butter and cheese

Ψαροκεφτέδες	*psarokeftethes*	Fish rissoles
Φασολάκια	*fasolakeea*	Green beans
Φέτα	*feta*	Tangy white cheese

Desserts

Βύσσινο γλυκό	*visino ghliko*	Cherry preserve
Γαλακτομπούρεκο	*ghalaktobooreeko*	Custard tart
Κανταΐφι	*kanda-eefee*	Filo pastry with honey and nuts
Λουκουμάδες	*lukumathes*	Honey-cinnamon doughnuts
Μπακλαβάς	*baklavas*	Filo pastry with honey and nuts
Μπισκότα	*biskota*	Biscuits
Νεγκόσκα	*negoska*	Red grapes
Πάστα	*pasta*	Gateau
Συκόπιτα	*sikopita*	Fig cake
Φράουλες	*fraooles*	Strawberries
Φρούτα	*froota*	Fruit

Dining on the verge

In the spring, Greeks collect wild greens by the roadside. These **chorta** appear in salads and pies, but are best steamed with a splash of lemon and olive oil.

Drinks

Αχαΐα Κλάους	*akhaeea klauss*	Peloponnesian vintage
Μπύρα	*bira*	Beer
Καφές ελληνικός	*kafes elinikos*	Greek coffee
- με γάλα	*- me ghala*	- with milk
- χωρίς γάλα	*- khoris ghala*	- without milk
- σκέτος	*- sketos*	- plain (no sugar)
- μέτριος	*- metrios*	- medium (some sugar)
- γλυκός	*- ghlikos*	- sweet
- χωρίς καφεΐνη	*- khoris kafeini*	- decaffeinated
- Φραπέ	*- frape*	- iced coffee

Café culture

Greek coffee – **kafe ellinikos** – has the strength of espresso, but with the grounds sludging the bottom of the cup. Borrow the bar's backgammon set – or buy your own wooden **tavli** board.

Κρητικός (οίνος)	kriteekos (eenos)	Cretan vintage
Κουμανταρία	kumandaria	Cypriot vintage
Μεταλλικό νερό	metaliko nero	Mineral water
- με ανθρακικό	- me anthrakiko	- sparkling
- χωρίς ανθρακικό	- khoris anthrakiko	- still
Μεταξά	metakhsa	Greek brandy
Νεμέας (οίνος)	nemeas (eenos)	Peloponnesian vintage
Ούζο	uzo	Ouzo: aniseed-flavoured spirit
Ρακί	raki	Village spirit, high in alcohol
Ρετσίνα	retsina	Pine-seasoned white wine
Τσάι με γάλα	tsai me ghala	Tea with milk
Τσάι από βότανα	tsai apo votana	Herbal tea
Τσίπουρο	tsipuro	Strong grape spirit
Χυμός μήλου	himos miloo	Apple juice

Snacks

Γιαούρτι	yaoortee	Yoghurt
Γύρος	yeeros	Doner kebab
Κουλούρι	kuluri	Sesame-coated pretzel
Μπουρέκια	boorekeea	Cypriot savoury puff pastry
Πασατέμπο	pasatempo	Pumpkin seeds
Πίτες	peetes	Savoury pies
Σπανακόπιτα	spanakopeeta	Spinach pie
Σουβλάκι	soovlakee	Meat kebab
Σάντουιτς	sanduits	Sandwich
Τυρόπιτα	tiropita	Cheese pie

Shopping

Athens is home to Tsakalof Street in the chi-chi Kolonaki district, reportedly rated among the six most expensive streets in the world. But the country's true character doesn't emerge here among the gilded laurel wreaths and accessory dogs. Instead, wander a **laiki agora** ('people's' or farmers' market). Each district hosts at least one weekly, peddling fresh fruits and vegetables, household goods and clothes. The capital's liveliest market can be found Saturday morning on Kallidromiou Street in Exarhia, a 20-minute walk from Syntagma Square.

Essentials

Where can I buy...?	Πού μπορώ να αγοράσω...;	pu boro na agoraso...?
I'd like to buy...	Θα ήθελα να αγοράσω...	tha ithela na aghoraso...
Do you have...?	Έχετε...;	ekhete...?
Do you sell...?	Πουλάτε...;	poolate...?
I'd like this...	Θα ήθελα αυτό...	tha ithela afto...
I'd prefer...	Προτιμώ...	protimo...
Could you show me...?	Μπορείτε να μου δείξετε...;	borite na mu thiksete...?
I'm just looking, thanks	Απλά κοιτάζω, ευχαριστώ	apla kitazo, efkhareesto
How much is it?	Πόσο κάνει;	poso kani?
Could you write down the price?	Μπορείτε να μου γράψετε την τιμή;	borite na mu ghrapsete tin timi?
Nothing else, thanks	Τίποτε άλλο, ευχαριστώ	tipote alo, efkhareesto
Do you accept credit cards?	Δέχεστε πιστωτική κάρτα;	theheste pistotiki karta?
It's a present, could I have it wrapped, please?	Είναι δώρο, μπορείτε να μου το τυλίξετε παρακαλώ;	ine thoro, borite na mu to tiliksete parakalo?
Could you post it to...?	Μπορείτε να το στείλετε στο...;	borite na to stilete sto...?
Can I exchange it?	Μπορώ να το αλλάζω;	boro na to alakso?
I'd like to return this	Θα ήθελα να επιστρέψω αυτό	tha ithela na epistrepso afto
I'd like a refund	Θα ήθελα επιστροφή χρημάτων	tha ithela epistrofi khrimaton

Local specialities

Greek souvenirs echo the country's long history. Most of its artisanal products could comfortably time-travel back a millennia or two: lace, baskets, pottery and jewellery, to name just a few. Two of the most distinctive products are ritualistic: **kompoloyia** (worry beads) and **filachto** (charms against the evil eye).

| Can you recommend a shop selling local specialities? | Μπορείτε να μου συστήσετε ένα κατάστημα με τοπικέςσπεσιαλιτέ; | borite na mu sistisete ena katastima me topikes specialite? |

What are the local specialities?	Ποιες είναι οι τοπικές σπεσιαλιτέ;	*pies ine i topikes specialite?*
What should I buy from here?	Τι θα μπορούσα να αγοράσω από εδώ;	*tee tha borusa na aghoraso apo edho?*
Is... (leather) good quality?	Είναι ... (το δέρμα) καλής ποιότητας;	*ine... (to dherma) kalis piotitas?*
Do you make the... (ceramics) yourself?	Κατασκευάζετε τα... (κεραμικά) ο ίδιος;	*kataskevazete ta... (keramika) o ithios?*
Is it handmade?	Είναι χειροποίητο;	*ine khiropi-ito?*
Do you make it to measure?	Το φτιάχνετε κατά παραγγελία;	*to ftiakhnete kata paranghelia?*
Can I order one?	Μπορώ να παραγγείλω ένα;	*boro na paraghilo ena?*

Beware of gifts

Flowers or pastries are appropriate presents for hosts if you're invited into a Greek home. Be careful not to admire any possession too much, or you'll take home that four-foot-tall Attic vase reproduction.

Popular things to buy

τάβλι	*tavli*	Backgammon board
καλάθια	*kalathia*	Baskets
μπρούτζινα είδη	*brudzina ithi*	Bronzeware
χαλιά	*khalia*	Carpets
μαξιλαροθήκες	*maksilarothikes*	Cushion covers
φυλαχτό	*filakhto*	Evil eye charm
εικόνες	*ikones*	Icons
κοσμήματα (χρυσά)	*kozmimata (khrisa)*	Jewellery (gold)
κοσμήματα (ασημένια)	*kozmimata (asimenia)*	Jewellery (silver)
δαντέλα	*thantela*	Lace
δερμάτινα είδη	*thermatina ithi*	Leatherwork
είδη αγγειοπλαστικής	*ithi agioplastikis*	Pottery
γλυπτά	*ghlipta*	Sculpture

| κομπολόγια | *koboloyia* | Worry beads |
| υφαντή τσάντα ώμου | *ifandi tsanda omu* | Woven shoulder bag |

Evil eye

Don't praise anything excessively; some Greeks believe this could draw evil spirits. Superstitious types spit or say "**ftou, ftou, ftou**". Cobalt charms, usually a flat staring eye, ward away the bad luck.

Clothes & shoes

Euro prices could be a smidgen lower than pounds, but, really, why bother with familiar chains? Instead, prowl Athens' Monstiraki flea market, just beside the Plaka, or wander the gilded streets of Kolonaki, where boutiques bloom. Notable local designers in the capital include Boutique Kostetsos (16 Levidou St), Lakis Gavalas Store (50 Voukourestiou St) and La Chrysotheque Zolotas (10 Panepistimiou St).

Where is the... department?	Που είναι το κατάστημα με τα...;	*pu ine to katastima me ta...?*
- clothes	- ρούχα	- *rookha*
- shoe	- παπούτσια	- *papootseea*
- women's	- γυναικεία	- *yeenekeea*
- men's	- ανδρικά	- *andreeka*
- children's	- παιδικά	- *pedeeka*
Which floor is the...?	Σε ποιον όροφο είναι...;	*se pion orofo ine...?*

I'm looking for...	Ψάχνω για...	*psakhno ya...*
- a skirt	- μια φούστα	- *mia foosta*
- trousers	- ένα παντελόνι	- *ena pandelonee*
- a top	- ένα μπλουζάκι	- *ena bloozakee*
- a jacket	- ένα μπουφάν	- *ena boofan*
- a T-shirt	- ένα t-shirt μπλουζάκι	- *ena tee-cert bloozakee*
- jeans	- ένα τζιν	- *ena jean*
- shoes	- παπούτσια	- *papootseea*
- underwear	- εσώρουχα	- *esorookha*

Can I try it on?	Μπορώ να το δοκιμάσω;	boro na to thokimaso?
What size is it?	Τι νούμερο είναι;	ti noomero ine?
My size is...	Το νούμερό μου είναι...	to noomero mu ine...
- small	- το μικρό (small)	- to mikro
- medium	- το μεσαίο (medium)	- to meseo
- large	- το μεγάλο (large)	- to meghalo

(see clothes size converter on p.96 for full range of sizes)

| Do you have this in my size? | Έχετε αυτό στο νούμερό μου; | ekhete afto sto noomero mu? |
| Where is the changing room? | Πού είναι τα δοκιμαστήρια; | pu ine ta dhokeemasteereea? |

It doesn't fit	Δεν μου κάνει	then mu kani
It doesn't suit me	Δεν μου πάει	then mu pai
Do you have a... size?	Έχετε ... νούμερο;	ekhete... noomero?
- bigger	- πιο μεγάλο	- pio meghalo
- smaller	- πιο μικρό	- pio mikro

Do you have it/ them in...	Έχετε αυτό/αυτά σε...	ekhete afto/afta se...
- black?	- μαύρο;	- mavro?
- white?	- άσπρο;	- aspro?
- blue?	- γαλάζιο;	- ghalazeeo?
- green?	- πράσινο;	- prasino?
- red?	- κόκκινο;	- kokeeno?

Are they made of leather?	Αυτά είναι φτιαγμένα από δέρμα;	afta ine ftiaghmena apo dherma?
I'm going to leave it/them	Δεν θα το/τα πάρω	dhen tha to/ta paro
I'll take it/them	Θα το/τα πάρω	tha to/ta paro

Athens' swish epicentre

Kolonaki teems with boutiques: Gucci, Lanvin, Bulgari, Lancel and Vuitton, to name a few. Tsakalof Street is the area's most famous thoroughfare.

You may hear...

Μπορώ να σας βοηθήσω;	boro na sas voithiso?	Can I help you?
Εξυπηρετείστε;	eksipiretiste?	Are you being served?
Ποιο νούμερο;	pio noomero?	What size?
Δεν έχουμε	dhen ekhume	We don't have any
Ορίστε	oriste	Here you are
Τίποτε άλλο;	tipote alo?	Anything else?
Να το τυλίξω;	na to tilikso?	Shall I wrap it for you?
Κάνει... (πενήντα) ευρώ	kani... (peninda) evro	It's... (50) euros
Έχει έκπτωση	ekhi ekptosi	It's reduced

Where to shop

Where can I find...	Πού μπορώ να βρω...	poo boro na vro...
- a bookshop?	- ένα βιβλιοπωλείο;	- ena veevleeopoleeo?
- a clothes shop?	- ένα κατάστημα ρούχων;	- ena katastima rookhon?
- a department store?	- ένα πολυκατάστημα;	- ena poleekatasteema?
- a gift shop?	- ένα κατάστημα δώρων;	- ena katastima dhoron?
- a music shop?	- ένα δισκάδικο;	- ena dhiskadhiko?
- a market?	- μία αγορά;	- mia aghora?

The Greek blues

Rembetika is a wildly popular mix of underworld ballads and Turkish orchestrations that developed in the 1920s hash dens of Piraeus. Stoa Athanaton hosts two performances daily in Athens' Central Market.

News and information

The International Herald Tribune includes a local news insert (www.ekathimerini.com). The English paper, the *Athens News*, is published on Fridays (www.athensnews.gr). Eleftheroudakis is Greece's oldest and largest foreign-language bookstore (17 Panepistimiou St, Athens; www.books.gr).

- a newsagent?	- ένα κατάστημα ψιλικών;	- *ena katastima psilikon?*
- a shoe shop?	- ένα κατάστημα με παπούτσια;	- *ena katastima me paputsia?*
- a souvenir shop?	- ένα κατάστημα με σουβενίρ;	- *ena katastima me souvenir?*
What's the best place to buy...?	Ποιο είναι το καλύτερο μέρος για να αγοράσω...;	*pio ine to kalitero meros ya na agoraso...?*
I'd like to buy...	Θα ήθελα...	*tha ithela...*
- a film	- ένα φιλμ	- *ena feelm*
- an English newspaper	- μια αγγλική εφημερίδα	- *mia anggliki efeemereedha*
- a map	- ένα χάρτη	- *ena kharti*
- postcards	- καρτ ποστάλ	- *kartpostal*
- a present	- ένα δώρο	- *ena dhoro*
- stamps	- γραμματόσημα	- *ghrammatoseema*
- sun cream	- ένα αντιηλιακό	- *ena andeeileeako*

Food & markets

| Is there a supermarket/ market nearby? | Πού είναι το πιο κοντινό σούπερ μάρκετ/αγορά; | *pu ine to pio kodino sooper market/aghora?* |

Can I have...	Μπορώ να έχω...	boro na echo...
- some bread?	- λίγο ψωμί;	- ligho psomee?
- some fruit?	- μερικά φρούτα;	- mereeka froota?
- some cheese?	- λίγο τυρί;	- ligho teeree?
- a bottle of water?	- ένα μπουκάλι νερό;	- ena bukali nero?
- a bottle of wine?	- ένα μπουκάλι κρασί;	- ena bukali krasi?

I'd like... of that	Θα ήθελα... από αυτό	tha ithela... apo afto
- half a kilo	- μισό κιλό	- miso kilo
- 250 grams	- διακόσια πενήντα γραμμάρια	- dhiakosia peninda ghramaria
- a small/big piece	- ένα μικρό/μεγάλο κομμάτι	- ena mikro/meghalo komati

Monastiraki flea market

Athenians throng the narrow alleyways and streets on the Plaka's edge, especially on Sundays. Bargaining is par for the course. The main shopping areas are Pandrossou and Ifaistou Streets near the Acropolis. Daily 9am-9pm.

Import & export

All prices include taxes, including the 19 per cent FPA, akin to VAT. Greece is extremely harsh on antiques smugglers. Organise documentation for any art – and be careful not to pocket debris at archaeological sites: that pot fragment could result in a hefty fine or even a prison term.

Getting around

Greece is a corrugated country, full of hairpin bends and steep mountains. Patience is required to travel here – and courage too. Road deaths jumped 51 per cent from 1980–2000, while they declined elsewhere in Europe.

The ferries and catamarans are the best island connections (flights are quite expensive, though prices are dropping as no-frill airlines expand). Bus transport is limited in resort areas, but usually geared towards tourists: with a bit of research, you'll be fine – and can enjoy a beachside ouzo with impunity.

Arrival

A sleek new airport, Eleftherios Venizelos, perches on the outskirts of Athens. Metro Line 3 finally links to the city, but the bus remains the cheapest option. Seafaring passengers arrive at Piraeus: catch Metro Line 1 or a bus to Syntagma. The port is vast, so visitors may not want to drag luggage to the public transport hubs; a cab costs €15-€20.

Where is/are the...	Πού είναι...	pu ine...
- luggage from flight...?	- οι αποσκευές από την πτήση...;	- ee aposkeves apo teen pteesee...?
- luggage trolleys?	- τα καροτσάκια για τις αποσκευές;	- ta karotsakia ya tees aposkeves?
- lost luggage office?	- το γραφείο απωλεσθέντων αντικειμένων;	- to ghrafeeo apolesthendon andeekeemenon?

Where is/are the...	Πού είναι...	pu ine...
- buses?	- τα λεωφορεία;	- ta leoforia?
- trains?	- τα τρένα;	- ta trena?
- taxis?	- τα ταξί;	- ta takhsi?
- car rental?	- το γραφείο ενοικίασης αυτοκινήτων;	- to ghrafeeo eneekeeasees aftokeeneeton?
- exit?	- η έξοδος;	- ee eksodhos?

How do I get to hotel...?	Πώς μπορώ να πάω στο ξενοδοχείο...;	pos boro na pao sto ksenotho-hio...?

My baggage is...	Οι αποσκευές μου έχουν...	i aposkeves mu ekhun...
- lost	- χαθεί	- khathi
- damaged	- πάθει ζημιά	- pathi zimia
- stolen	- κλαπεί	- klapi

Customs

Officials sometimes wave EU nationals through, but be polite, attentive and straightforward if questioned (no funny stuff). Avoid visiting if you have a passport stamp from the Turkish Republic of Northern Cyprus, which the international community considers an occupied territory, not a country. You could be denied entry. However, since Cyprus joined the European Union, the practice is waning.

The children are on this passport	Τα παιδιά είναι σ'αυτό το διαβατήριο	ta *pethia* *ine* *safto* to *thiavatirio*
We're here on holiday	Είμαστε εδώ για διακοπές	*imaste* *etho* ya thi-*akopes*
I'm going to...	Πηγαίνω στο...	*piyeno* sto...
I have nothing to declare	Δεν έχω τίποτε να δηλώσω	den *ekho* *tipote* na *thiloso*
Do I have to declare this?	Πρέπει να το δηλώσω αυτό;	*prepi* na to *thiloso* *afto*?

Car hire

Rentals in Greece can be wincingly expensive. Expect to pay at least €250–€300 per week from companies such as Avance or Capital. The rates double at multinational chains. Most have airport kiosks, as well as central locations in the capital (clustered on Syngrou, near the Acropolis Metro stop). Greek-owned easyCar may be able to slash prices.

I'd like to hire a...	Θα ήθελα να νοικιάσω ένα...	tha *eethela* na *neekyaso* *ena*...
- car	- αυτοκίνητο	- *aftokeeneto*
- people carrier	- πολυμορφικό όχημα	- *poleemorfiko* *okheema*
with...	με...	*me*...
- air conditioning	- κλιματιστικό	- *kleemateesteeko*
- automatic transmission	- αυτόματο κιβώτιο ταχυτήτων	- *aftomato* kee*vo-teeo* takhee*teeton*

Goodbye smog and smoke

The capital's notorious **nefos** (smog) has decreased by 35 per cent, thanks to traffic-calming measures and better emission controls. Tourists are breathing a sigh of relief too, as non-smoking sections become mandatory.

How much is that for a...	Πόσο κοστίζει αυτό για μία...	poso kosteezee afto ya meea...
- day?	- μέρα;	- mera?
- week?	- εβδομάδα;	- evdhomadha?
Does that include...	Αυτό συμπεριλαμβάνει...	afto siberilamvani...
- mileage?	- τη χιλιομετρική κάλυψη;	- tee kheeliometree-kee kaleepsee?
- insurance?	- την ασφάλεια;	- teen asfaleea?

On the road

The Greeks are Mediterranean drivers: fast, flash and more fatal than most. Laws are just serving suggestions, though the police now ticket triple-parked vehicles in the capital. Still, expect to see vehicles passing wildly on the centreline and verge. On national holidays, some motorway lanes reverse to hasten Athenlan traffic; also watch for non-operational traffic lights – and police directing the chaos.

What is the speed limit?	Ποιο είναι το όριο ταχύτητας;	pio eene to orio tahititas?
Can I park here?	Μπορω να παρκάρω εδώ;	boro na parkaro etho?
Where is a petrol station?	Πού είναι ένα πρατήριο βενζίνης;	Pu ine ena pratirio venzinees?
Please fill up the tank with...	Γεμίστε το παρακαλώ με...	yemiste to parakalo me...
- unleaded	- αμόλυβδη	- amolivthee
- diesel	- ντίζελ	- dizel
- leaded	- μολυβδούχα	- molivthukha
- LPG	- υγραέριο LPG	- ighraerio LPG

Directions

Is this the road to...?	Αυτός ο δρόμος πάει προς...;	aftos o thromos paee pros...?
How do I get to...?	Πώς μπορώ να πάω στο...;	pos boro na pao sto...?
How far is it to...?	Πόσο μακριά είναι ο/η/το m/f/n...;	poso makria ine o/ee/to...?
How long will it take?	Πόσο διαρκεί το ταξίδι;	poso thiarki to taksithi?
Could you point it out on the map?	Μπορείτε να μου το δείξετε στο χάρτη;	borite na mu to thiksete sto kharti?
I've lost my way	Έχω χαθεί	echo khathi
On the right/left	στα δεξιά/αριστερά	sta theksia/aristera

Turn right/left	Στρίψτε δεξιά/ αριστερά	*stripste theksia/ aristera*
Straight ahead	Ευθεία	*eftheea*
Turn around	Γυρίστε πίσω	*gheereeste peeso*

Public transport

Athens spruced up its metro system before the 2004 Olympics – and it continues to dazzle. Purchase either an **aplo** (single ticket) or an **imerisio eisitirio** (all-day ticket), valid on trams, buses and the underground. Punch the ticket through a validating machine – often yellow – the first time you use it.

Going underground

The Athenian metro boasts 19 new state-of-the art stations, which are clean, bright and efficient. The ruins and relics disturbed by the construction are on display.

Bus	Λεωφορείο	*leoforio*
Bus station	Σταθμός λεωφορείων	*stathmos leoforion*
Train	Τρένο	*treno*
Train station	Σιδηροδρομικός σταθμός	*seedheerodromeekos stathmos*
I would like to go to...	Θα ήθελα να πάω στο...	*tha eethela na pao sto...*
I would like a... ticket	Θα ήθελα ένα εισιτήριο...	*tha eethela ena isi-tirio...*
- single	- απλό	*- aplo*
- return	- μετά επιστροφής	*- meta epistrofis*
- first class	- πρώτης θέσης	*- protis thesis*
- smoking/non-smoking	- στους καπνίζοντες/ στους μη καπνίζοντες	*- stus kapnizodes/ stus mi kapnizodes*
What time does it leave/arrive?	Τι ώρα φεύγει/φτάνει;	*ti ora fevyi/ftanee?*

| Could you tell me when we get to...? | Παρακαλώ πέστε μου όταν φτάσουμε στο...; | parakalo peste mu otan ftasume sto...? |

Taxis

Taxi drivers are notorious here – for price-inflation, poor navigation skills and reluctance to stop. Unless it's an emergency, take public transport.

I'd like a taxi to...	Θα ήθελα ένα ταξί για...	tha ithela ena taksi ya...
How much is it to the...	Πόσο κοστίζει έως το...	poso kosteezee eos to...
- airport?	- αεροδρόμιο;	- aerodromio?
- town centre?	- κέντρο;	- kentro?
- hotel?	- ξενοδοχείο;	- ksenothohio?

Tours

Athenian attractions cluster mainly around the Acropolis. New pedestrian walkways make independent touring quite pleasant. However, in the dull heat of summer, a bus tour may gain appeal. Outside the city, walking tours remain popular, along with the more adventurous (waterskiing, scubadiving) and esoteric (yoga, retreats for men with the Mt Athos monks). Regardless of location, if you opt for an archaeological tour, make sure the leader belongs to the Union of Official Guides.

Are there any organised tours?	Υπάρχουν οργανωμένες περιηγήσεις;	eeparkhun orghanomenes peri-iyisis?
Where do they leave from?	Από πού ξεκινούν;	apo pu ksekinun?
What time does it start?	Τι ώρα ξεκινά;	tee ora ksekina?
Do you have English-speaking guides?	Έχετε αγγλόφωνους ξεναγούς;	ekhete anglofonus ksenaghus?
Is lunch/tea included?	Περιλαμβάνεται το μεσημεριανό γεύμα;	perilamvanete to mesimeriano yevma?
Do we get any free time?	Θα έχουμε καθόλου ελεύθερο χρόνο;	tha ekhume katholu eleftithero chrono?
Are we going to see...?	Θα δούμε...;	tha dume...?
What time do we get back?	Τι ώρα επιστρέφουμε;	tee ora epistrefume?

Accommodation

While Greece has some lovely posh properties, overall accommodation is more functional than fantastic. Perhaps that's due to the lively street culture. Locals go out – and expect visitors to do the same. Why spend hard-earned euros on mini-bars or high-thread-count sheets, when you could dance in a seaside disco, play backgammon in a sunny **plateia** (town square) or share fresh octopus and copper pitchers of local wine with friends? At any rate, in some rural areas, luxury simply isn't an option. Bring your own towel and soap – and explore!

Types of accommodation

Urban hotel prices escalate quickly, especially in Athens. A-class hotels are luxurious, of course. B-class ones have private bathrooms and constant hot water. C-class straggle behind. Expect to share a loo in the D-bracket and suffer the odd cold shower. E-class may not heat water at all.

Consider a private single or double in a hostel instead. Budget travellers can also seek out a **dwmatio** (room for rent). Most don't have kitchenettes, but in-room picnics are permissible.

I'd like to stay in...	Θα ήθελα να μείνω σε...	tha _ithela na _meeno se..._
- an apartment	- διαμέρισμα	- thia_merizma_
- a campsite	- κάμπινγκ	- _kamping_
- a hotel	- ξενοδοχείο	- ksenotho_hio_
- rented room	- ενοικιαζόμενο δωμάτιο	- eneekcea_zomeno_ _thomatio_
- a youth hostel	- ξενώνα νεότητας	- ksе_nona_ ne-_o-teetas_
- a guest house	- πανσιόν	- pan_sion_

Is it...	Είναι...	_ine..._
- full board?	- με πλήρη διατροφή;	- me _pliree_ thiatro_fi_?
- half board?	- με ημιδιατροφή;	- me imithiatro_fi_?
- self-catering?	- αυτοτροφοδοτούμενο;	- aftotrofotho-_too_meno?

Mosquito coast

Pack insect repellent and some deterrent. The incense-like coil can trigger headaches and fears of fire; try the electric plug types instead. A small fan, pointed at the bed, also works well.

Reservations

Do you have any rooms available?	Έχετε διαθέσιμα δωμάτια;	*ekhete dheeathe-seema dhomateea?*
Can you recommend anywhere else?	Έχετε να προτείνετε κάτι άλλο;	*echete na pro-teenete katee alo?*
I'd like to make a reservation for...	Θα ήθελα να κλείσω ένα δωμάτιο για...	*tha ithela na kliso ena dhomateeo yia...*
- tonight	- απόψε	- *apopse*
- one night	- ένα βράδυ	- *ena vradhee*
- two nights	- δύο βράδια	- *thio vradheea*
- a week	- μία εβδομάδα	- *meea evthomatha*
From... (May 1st) to... (May 8th)	Από τις... (1 Μαΐου) μέχρι τις... (8 Μαΐου)	*apo tis (meea maeeoo) mekhri tis (okhto maeeoo)*

Room types

Cuddly couples should specify a **diplo krevati** (double bed), or face two singles. Greece spruced up its accommodation substantially before the 2004 Olympics, but services still lag behind the mod-cons of northern Europe. Don't let this bother you. The culture is all about going out, so location is more important than a trouser press, unless you're travelling on business.

Do you have... room?	Έχετε ένα... δωμάτιο;	*ekhete ena... dhomateeo?*
- a single	- μονόκλινο	- *monokleeno*
- a double	- δίκλινο	- *thikleeno*
- a family	- οικογενειακό	- *eekoyeneeako*
with...	με...	*me...*
- a cot?	- παιδικό κρεβάτι;	- *pethiko krevati?*
- twin beds?	- δύο κρεβάτια;	- *thio krevatia?*
- a double bed?	- διπλό κρεβάτι;	- *thiplo krevati?*
- a bath/shower?	- μπάνιο/ντους;	- *banio/dous?*
- air conditioning?	- κλιματιστικό;	- *kleematisteeko?*
- internet access?	- πρόσβαση στο διαδίκτυο;	- *prosvasee sto thiathiktio?*
Can I see the room?	Μπορώ να δω το δωμάτιο;	*boro na tho to dhomateeo?*

45

Prices

Prices fluctuate according to season and savvy: always ask about special offers, corporate discounts and Internet rates, which might trim 25-50 per cent off the bill. By law, hotels must post service information on the room door, detailing prices, check-out time and extras (like breakfast). Accommodation tax is high, but hidden in the bill. Tipping isn't widespread here, but shell out in swisher establishments: €1-2 for a porter, €3 for a concierge or maid.

How much is...	Πόσο κοστίζει...	_poso kosteezee..._
- a double room?	- ένα δίκλινο δωμάτιο;	- _ena dheekleeno dhomateeo?_
- per night?	- ανά βραδιά;	- _ana vradheea?_
- per week?	- ανά εβδομάδα;	- _ana evthomatha?_
Is breakfast included?	Το πρωινό συμπεριλαμβάνεται στην τιμή;	_to proeeno seempereelamvanete steen teemee?_
Is there...	Υπάρχει...	_eeparchee..._
- a swimming pool?	- πισίνα;	- _pisina?_
- a lift?	- ασανσέρ;	- _asanser?_
I'll take it	Θα το κλείσω	_tha to kleeso_
Can I pay by...	Μπορώ να πληρώσω με...	_boro na pliroso me..._
- credit card?	- πιστωτική κάρτα;	- _pistotiki karta?_
- traveller's cheque?	- ταξιδιωτική επιταγή;	- _taksithiotiki epitayi?_

BYO
Budget travellers should seek out **enoikiazomena dwmatia** (room rentals). Pack a towel and soap, as many families don't supply basics.

Special requests

Could you...	Μπορείτε να...	_borite na..._
- put this in the hotel safe?	- βάλετε αυτό στο χρηματοκιβώτιο του ξενοδοχείου;	- _valete afto sto chreematokeevoteeo tou ksenodhocheeou?_

Athens' grande dame
The Hotel Grande Bretagne has welcomed royalty, celebrities and spies for 130 years. Revived by an €82m makeover for the Olympics, it nearly outshines the neighbouring Parliament building (www.grandebretagne.gr).

- order a taxi for me?	- καλέσετε ένα ταξί;	- *kalesete ena taksi?*
- wake me up at (7am)?	- με ξυπνήσετε στις (7 το πρωί);	- *me ksipnisete stis (efta to proee)?*
Can I have a...	Μπορώ να έχω ένα...	*boro na ekho ena...*
- room with a sea view?	- δωμάτιο με θέα στη θάλασσα;	- *dhomateeo me thea stee thalasa?*
- bigger room?	- μεγαλύτερο δωμάτιο;	- *meghaleetero dhomateeo?*
- quieter room?	- πιο ήσυχο δωμάτιο;	- *pio isikho dhomateeo?*
Is there...	Υπάρχει...	*eeparchee...*
- a safe?	- χρηματοκιβώτιο;	- *khrimatokivotio?*
- a babysitting service?	- μπέιμπι σίτερ;	- *beibi siter?*
- a laundry service?	- υπηρεσία πλυντηρίου;	- *ipiresia plidiriu?*
Is there wheelchair access?	Υπάρχει πρόσβαση για αναπηρικές καρέκλες;	*iparhi prosvasee ya anapirikes karekles?*

Checking in & out

I have a reservation for tonight	Έχω κάνει μια κράτηση για απόψε	ekho kani meea kratisi ya apopse
In the name of...	Είναι στο όνομα...	ine sto onoma...
Here's my passport	Αυτό είναι το διαβατήριό μου	afto ine to thiavatirio mu
What time is check out?	Τι ώρα είναι η αναχώρηση;	ti ora ine ee anakhorisi?
Can I have a later check out?	Μπορώ να φύγω πιο αργά;	boro na figho pio argha?
Can I leave my bags here?	Μπορώ να αφήσω τις βαλίτσες μου εδώ;	boro na afiso tis valitses mu etho?
I'd like to check out	Θα ήθελα να αναχωρήσω τώρα	tha eethela na anachoreeso tora
Can I have the bill?	Μπορώ να έχω το λογαριασμό;	boro na echo to loghariazmo?

Camping

Do you have...	Έχετε...	ekhete...
- a site available?	- ελεύθερο χώρο;	- elefthero khoro?
- electricity?	- ηλεκτρισμό;	- elektrizmo?
- hot showers?	- εγκαταστάσεις για ζεστό ντους;	- egatastasis ya zesto duz?
- tents for hire?	- ενοικιαζόμενες σκηνές;	- eneekeeazomenes skeenes?
How much is it per...	Πόσο κοστίζει ανά...	poso kostizi ana...
- tent?	- σκηνή;	- skeenee?
- caravan?	- τροχόσπιτο;	- trokhospito?
- person?	- άτομο;	- atomo?
- car?	- αυτοκίνητο;	- aftokinito?
Where is/are the...	Πού είναι...	pu ine...
- reception?	- η ρεσεψιόν;	- ee resepseeon?
- bathrooms?	- τα μπάνια;	- ta baneea?
- laundry facilities?	- οι εγκαταστάσεις πλυντηρίου;	- ee egatastasis pleedeerioo?

Survival guide

Shops operate at odd hours, take
blurry, long lunch breaks and
generally shutter Saturday at noon
until Monday morning. In a fix,
remember that kiosks are like
magicians' hats, unpacking a wealth
of goods, including beer, aspirin
and stamps.

Greece has many Internet cafés,
largely populated by chain-smoking
teen gamers. Locals – especially in
less-touristy areas – take pride in
helping visitors. Muster all the Greek
you can, though, as they're not likely
to speak much English (French or
Italian are often good alternatives).

Money & banks

Where is the nearest...	Πού είναι η πιο κοντινή... f	pu ine i pio kodinee/
	Πού είναι το πιο κοντινό... n	pu ine to pio kodino...
- bank?	- τράπεζα; f	- trapeza?
- ATM/bank machine?	- αυτόματο μηχάνημα ανάληψης χρημάτων (ΑΤΜ); n	- aftomato michaneema analeepsees chreematon (ATM)?
- foreign exchange office?	- γραφείο αλλαγής χρημάτων; n	- ghrafio alaghees khrimaton?
I'd like to...	Θα ήθελα να...	tha ithela na...
- withdraw money	- αποσύρω χρήματα	- aposiro khrimata
- cash a traveller's cheque	- εξαργυρώσω μια ταξιδιωτική επιταγή	- eksargheeroso mia taksithiotiki epitaghee
- change money	- αλλάξω χρήματα	- alakso khrimata
- arrange a transfer	- κανονίσω μια μεταφορά χρημάτων	- kanoniso mia metafora khrimaton
Could I have smaller notes, please?	Θα ήθελα πιο μικρά χαρτονομίσματα παρακαλώ;	tha ithela pio mikra khartonomismata parakalo?
What's the exchange rate?	Ποια είναι η τιμή συναλλάγματος;	pia ine i timi seenalaghmatos?
What's the commission?	Ποια είναι η προμήθεια;	pia ine ee promeetheea?
What's the charge for...	Ποια είναι η χρέωση για να...	pia ine i khreosi yia na...
- making a withdrawal	- αποσύρω χρήματα	- aposiro khrimata
- exchanging money	- αλλάξω χρήματα	- alakso khrimata
- cashing a cheque	- εξαργυρώσω μια ταξιδιωτική επιταγή	- eksargheeroso mia taksithiotiki epitaghee
This is not right	Αυτό δεν είναι σωστό	afto dhen ine sosto
Is there a problem with my account?	Υπάρχει πρόβλημα με το λογαριασμό μου;	iparhi provlima me to loghariasmo mu?
The ATM/bank machine took my card	Το αυτόματο μηχάνημα ανάληψης χρημάτων κράτησε την κάρτα μου	to aftomato mikhanima analeepsees khrimaton kratise tin karta mu
I've forgotten my PIN	Ξέχασα τον κωδικό PIN μου	ksehasa ton kothiko PIN mu

Going postal
Greeks multitask at the post office, paying bills, receiving pensions, managing their savings accounts and so on. Skip the queues and buy stamps from news kiosks instead.

Post office

Where is the (main) post office?	Πού είναι το (κεντρικό) ταχυδρομείο;	pu _ine_ to (kendriko) takheedhrom_ee_o?
I'd like to send ...	Θα ήθελα να στείλω...	tha _ithela_ na _steelo_...
- a letter	- ένα γράμμα	- _ena ghrama_
- a postcard	- μια κάρτα	- mia _karta_
- a parcel	- ένα δέμα	- _ena thema_
- a fax	- ένα φαξ	- _ena_ faks
I'd like to send this...	Θα ήθελα να στείλω αυτό...	tha _ithela_ na _steelo afto_...
- to the United Kingdom	- στο Ηνωμένο Βασίλειο	- sto inom_eno_ vas_ee_leeo
- by airmail	- αεροπορικώς	- aeropori_kos_
- by express mail	- εξπρές	- eks_pres_
- by registered mail	- συστημένο	- sisti_meno_
I'd like...	Θα ήθελα...	tha _ithela_...
- a stamp for this letter/postcard	- ένα γραμματόσημο για αυτό το γράμμα/ αυτή την κάρτα	- _ena_ ghramat_osimo_ ya af_to_ to _ghrama_/ af_ti_ teen _karta_
- to buy envelopes	- να αγοράσω ένα φάκελο	- na agho_raso ena fakelo_
- to make a photocopy	- να κάνω μία φωτοτυπία	- na _kano_ mia fototip_eea_
It's fragile	Είναι εύθραυστο	_ine_ efthrafsto

Telecoms

Where can I make an international phone call?	Πού μπορώ να κάνω μία διεθνή κλήση;	pu boro na kano mia dhiethnee kleesee?
Where can I buy a phonecard?	Πού μπορώ να αγοράσω μια τηλεκάρτα;	pu boro na aghoraso mia tilekarta?
How do I call abroad?	Πώς μπορώ να πάρω τηλέφωνο στο εξωτερικό;	pos boro na paro teelefono sto eksoteriko?
How much does it cost per minute?	Πόσο κοστίζει ανά λεπτό;	poso kostizi ana lepto?
The number is...	Ο αριθμός είναι...	o arithmos ine...
What's the area/country code for...?	Ποιος είναι ο κωδικός της περιοχής/της χώρας για...;	pios ine o kothikos tees periokhees/tees khoras ya...?
The number is engaged	Είναι κατειλημμένο	ine katilimeno
The connection is bad	Η σύνδεση είναι κακή	i sinthesi ine kaki
I've been cut off	Η σύνδεση διεκόπηκε	i sindhesi diekopeeke
I'd like...	Θα ήθελα...	tha ithela...
- a charger for my mobile phone	- ένα φορτιστή για το τηλέφωνό μου	- ena fortisti ya to tilefono mu
- an adaptor plug	- ένα μετατροπέα	- ena metatropea
- a pre-paid SIM card	- μία προπληρωμένη κάρτα SIM	- mia propleeromenee karta sim

Cheap calls

Buy a Greek SIM card for your mobile phone. A local number will be yours for the duration of your stay, the cost of local calls and texting come down considerably, and incoming calls are free.

Trapped in the net

Internet cafés dot the country. Even remote villages have connections, mainly because teenage boys need a place to smoke and scream at PC games. Count on access... just not the most pleasant ambience.

Internet

Where's the nearest Internet café?	Πού είναι το πιο κοντινό ίντερνετ καφέ;	*pu ine to pio kodhi-no internet kafe?*
Can I access the Internet here?	Μπορώ να έχω πρόσβαση στο ίντερνετ;	*boro na ekho pros-vasi sto internet?*
I'd like to...	Θα ήθελα...	*tha ithela...*
- use the Internet	- να έχω πρόσβαση στο ίντερνετ	*- na ekho prosvasi sto internet*
- check my email	- να ελέγχω το ημέιλ/email μου	*- na elengso to imeil mu*
- use a printer	- να χρησιμοποιήσω έναν εκτυπωτή	*- na khrisimopi-iso enan ektipoti*
How much is it...	Πόσο κοστίζει...	*poso kostizi...*
- per minute?	- ανά λεπτό;	*- ana lepto?*
- per hour?	- ανά ώρα;	*- ana ora?*
- to buy a CD?	- ένα CD;	*- ena CD?*
How do I...	Πώς...	*pos...*
- log on?	- συνδέομαι;	*- seendheome?*
- open a browser?	- ανοίγω το φυλλομετρητή/ browser;	*- aneegho to filometriti/brauser?*
- print this?	- μπορώ να εκτυπώσω αυτό;	*- boro na ektiposo afto?*
I need help with this computer	Χρειάζομαι βοήθεια με αυτόν τον υπολογιστή	*khriazome voeetheea me afton ton ipologhistee*

| The computer has crashed | Αυτός ο υπολογιστής κράσαρε | aftos o ipologistees krasare |
| I've finished | Τελείωσα | teliosa |

Chemist

| Where's the nearest (all-night) pharmacy? | Πού είναι το πιο κοντινό (διανυκτερεύον) φαρμακείο; | pu ine to pio kodino (dianikterevon) farmakio? |
| What time does the pharmacy open/close? | Πότε ανοίγει/κλείνει το φαρμακείο; | pote aneeyee/kleenee to farmakio? |

I need something for...	Χρειάζομαι κάτι για...	khriazome kati ya...
- diarrhoea	- τη διάρροια	- tee thiaria
- a cold	- το κρύωμα	- to krioma
- a cough	- το βήχα	- to vikha
- insect bites	- τσίμπημα από έντομο	- tsibima apo edomo
- sunburn	- ηλιακό έγκαυμα	- iliako egavma
- motion sickness	- τη ναυτία	- tee naftia
- hay fever	- το αλλεργικό συνάχι	- to aleryiko sinakhi
- period pain	- τον πόνο περιόδου	- ton pono periothu
- abdominal pains	- τον κοιλόπονο	- ton kilopono
- a urine infection	- ουρολοίμωξη	- uroleemoksi
- a vaginal infection	- κολπική μόλυνση	- kolpiki molinsi

I'd like...	Θα ήθελα ...	tha ithela...
- aspirin	- ασπιρίνη	- aspirini
- plasters	- λευκοπλάστ	- lefkoplast
- condoms	- προφυλακτικά	- profilaktika
- insect repellent	- ένα εντομοαπωθητικό	- ena edomoapothitiko
- painkillers	- παυσίπονα	- pafsipona
- a contraceptive	- αντισυλληπτικά	- adisiliptika

How much should I take?	Πόσο να πάρω;	poso na paro?
Take..	Πάρε...	pare...
- a tablet	- μία ταμπλέτα	- mia tableta
- a teaspoon	- ένα κουταλάκι του γλυκού	- ena kutalaki tu gliku
- with water	- με νερό	- me nero

How often should I take this?	Πόσο συχνά να το παίρνω;	*poso sikhna* na to *perno?*
- once/twice a day	- μία φορά/δύο φορές την ημέρα	- *mia fora/thio fores tin eemera*
- before/after meals	πριν/μετά από τα γεύματα	- *prin/meta apo ta yevmata*
- in the morning/ evening	- το πρωί/το απόγευμα	- *to proee/to apoyevma*
Is it suitable for children?	Είναι κατάλληλο για παιδιά;	*ine katalilo ya pethia?*
Will it make me drowsy?	Θα μου φέρει υπνηλία;	*tha mu feri ipnilia?*
Do I need a prescription?	Χρειάζομαι συνταγή;	*khriazome sidayi?*
I have a prescription	Έχω συνταγή	*ekho sidayi*

Children

Where should I take the children?	Πού μπορώ να πάω τα παιδιά;	*pu boro na pao ta pethia?*
Where is the nearest...	Πού είναι ο/η πιο κοντινός/ή...	*pu ine o/i pio kodinos/i...*
- playground?	- παιδική χαρά;	- *pethiki khara?*
- fairground?	- λούνα παρκ;	- *luna park?*
- zoo?	- ζωολογικός κήπος;	- *zo-ooloyikos kipos?*
- swimming pool?	- πισίνα;	- *pisina?*
- park?	- πάρκο;	- *parko?*
Is this suitable for children?	Αυτό είναι κατάλληλο για παιδιά;	*afto ine katalilo ya pethia?*
Are children allowed?	Επιτρέπονται τα παιδιά;	*epitreponde ta pethia?*
Are there baby-changing facilities here?	Υπάρχει εδώ δωμάτιο για άλλαγμα μωρών;	*iparhi edo thomatio ya alaghma moron?*
Do you have...	Έχετε...	*ekhete...*
- a children's menu?	- μενού για παιδιά;	- *menu yia pethia?*
- a high chair?	- παιδική καρέκλα;	- *pethiki karekla?*
Is there...	Υπάρχει...	*iparhi...*
- a child-minding service?	- υπηρεσία φύλαξης παιδιών;	- *ipiresia filaksis pethion?*
- a nursery?	- παιδικός σταθμός;	- *pethikos stathmos?*

Can you recommend a reliable babysitter?	Μπορείτε να μου συστήσετε μια αξιόπιστη μπέημπι σίτερ;	borite na mu sistisete mia aksiopisti beibi siter?
Are the children constantly supervised?	Τα παιδιά επιτηρούνται συνεχώς;	ta pethia epitirunde sinekhos?
When can I bring them?	Πότε μπορώ να τα φέρω;	pote boro na ta fero?
What time do I have to pick them up?	Τι ώρα πρέπει να τα παραλάβω;	tee ora prepee na ta paralavo?
He/she is... years old	Αυτός/αυτή είναι ... χρονών	aftos/afti ine... khronon
I'd like to buy...	Θα ήθελα να αγοράσω...	tha ithela na aghoraso...
- nappies	- πάνες	- panes
- baby wipes	- υγρά μωρομάντηλα	- ighra moromandila
- tissues	- χαρτομάντηλα	- khartomandila

Travellers with disabilities

I have a disability	Έχω μια αναπηρία	ekho mia anapiria
I need assistance	Χρειάζομαι βοήθεια	khriazome voithia
I am blind	Είμαι τυφλός/ή m/f	ime tiflos/i
I am deaf	Είμαι κουφός/ή m/f	ime kufos/i
I have a hearing aid	Έχω ακουστικά	ekho akustika
I can't walk well	Δεν περπατώ καλά	dhen perpato kala
Is there a lift?	Υπάρχει ασανσέρ;	iparhi asanser?
Is there wheelchair access?	Υπάρχει πρόσβαση για αναπηρικές καρέκλες;	iparhi prosvasi yia anapirikes karekles?
Can I bring my guide dog?	Επιτρέπονται τα σκυλιά-οδηγοί για τυφλούς;	epitrepontai ta skilia-odhiyi ya tiflus?
Are there disabled toilets?	Υπάρχουν τουαλέτες για άτομα με αναπηρία;	iparkhun tualetes yia atoma me anapiria?
Do you offer disabled services?	Έχετε υπηρεσίες για άτομα με αναπηρία;	ekhete ipiresies ya atoma me anapiria?
Could you help me...	Μπορείτε να με βοηθήσετε να...	borite na me voithisete na...
- cross the street?	- περάσω το δρόμο;	- peraso to thromo?
- go up/down the stairs?	- ανέβω/κατέβω τις σκάλες;	- anevo/katevo tis skales?

Can I sit down somewhere?	Μπορώ να καθίσω κάπου;	*boro na kathiso kapu?*
Could you call a disabled taxi for me?	Μπορείτε να καλέσετε ένα ταξί για άτομα με αναπηρία;	*borite na kalesete ena taksi ya atoma me anapiria?*

Repairs & cleaning

This is broken	Αυτό έχει χαλάσει	*afto ekhi halasi*
Can you fix it?	Μπορείτε να το διορθώσετε;	*borite na to dhiorthosete?*
Do you have...	Έχετε...	*ekhete...*
- batteries?	- μπαταρίες;	*- bataries?*
- spare parts?	- ανταλλακτικά;	*- antalaktika?*
Can you... this?	Μπορείτε να... αυτό;	*borite na... afto?*
- clean	- καθαρίσετε	*- katharisete*
- press	- σιδερώσετε	*- siderosete*
- dry-clean	- στεγνοκαθαρίσετε	*- steghnokatharisete*
- patch	- μπαλώσετε	*- balosete*
When will it be ready?	Πότε θα είναι έτοιμο;	*pote tha ine etimo?*
This isn't mine	Δεν είναι δικό μου	*dhen ine diko mu*

Survival guide

Matt Barrett – a travel portal pioneer – has become an institution: Athenians even suggested the American resident run for mayor in 2000. www.athensguide.com remains the go-to site, despite its somewhat dated design.

Tourist information

Where's the Tourist Information Office?	Πού είναι το γραφείο τουρισμού;	*pu ine to ghrafio turismu?*
Do you have a city/regional map?	Έχετε ένα χάρτη της πόλης/της περιοχής;	*ekhete ena kharti tis polis/tis periokhis?*

What are the main places of interest?	Ποια είναι τα κύρια μέρη ενδιαφέροντος;	pia ine ta kiria meri endiaferondos?
Could you show me on the map?	Μπορείτε να μου δείξετε στο χάρτη;	borite na mu thiksete sto kharti?
We'll be here for...	Είμαστε εδώ για...	imaste etho ya...
- half a day	- μισή ημέρα	- misi imera
- a day	- μια ημέρα	- mia imera
- a week	- μια εβδομάδα	- mia evthomatha
Do you have a brochure in English?	Έχετε το φυλλάδιο στα αγγλικά;	ekhete to filadhio sta angglika?
We're interested in...	Θα μας ενδιέφερε.../ Θα μας ενδιέφεραν...	tha mas endiefere.../ tha mas endieferan...
- history	- η ιστορία	- ee istoreea
- architecture	- η αρχεκτονική	- ee architektoniki
- shopping	- τα ψώνια	- ta psonia
- hiking	- η πεζοπορία	- ee pezoporeea
- a scenic walk	- ένας γραφικός περίπατος	- enas ghrafikos peripatos
- a boat cruise	- μια κρουαζιέρα	- mia kruaziera
- a guided tour	- μία περιήγηση με ξεναγό	- mia peri-iyisi me ksenagho
Are there any excursions?	Υπάρχουν οργανωμένες εκδρομές;	eeparkhoon orghanomenes ekdhromes?
How long does it take?	Πόση ώρα διαρκεί;	posi ora thiarki?
What does it cost?	Πόσο κάνει;	poso kanee?
What days is it open/closed?	Ποιες ημέρες είναι ανοικτό/κλειστό;	poies imeres ine aneekto/kleesto?
What time does it open/close?	Τι ώρα ανοίγει/κλείνει;	tee ora aneeyee/kleenee?
What's the admission price?	Πόσο κοστίζει η είσοδος;	poso kostizi ee isothos?
Are there any tours in English?	Κάνετε περιηγήσεις στα αγγλικά;	kanete peri-iyisis sta angglika?

Emergencies

Greece is relatively safe – in that pickpocket-but-not-mugging way common in the Mediterranean. Guard against thieves around Athens' Omonia Square late at night, however.

The nation is fairly comfortable: medical facilities work and tap water is safe (though heavily chlorinated). Urban smog may aggravate asthma and allergies: pack remedies.

The age limit for drinking, smoking and driving in Greece is 18. Public drunkenness is frowned upon, though. Plan around siestas – 2pm–5.30pm in summer – and cover your limbs in churches to avoid tension with locals.

Medical

Where is the...	Πού είναι το...	*pu ine to...*
- hospital?	- νοσοκομείο;	*- nosokomio?*
- health centre?	- κέντρο υγείας;	*- kedro eegheeas?*
I need...	Χρειάζομαι...	*khriazome...*
- a doctor	- ένα γιατρό	*- ena yiatro*
- a female doctor	- μια γυναίκα γιατρό	*- mia yineka yiatro*
- an ambulance	- ένα ασθενοφόρο	*- ena asthenoforo*
It's very urgent	Είναι πολύ επείγον	*ine pole epeeghon*
I'm injured	Έχω τραυματιστεί	*ekho travmatisti*
Can I see the doctor?	Μπορώ να δω ένα γιατρό;	*boro na tho ena yiatro?*
I don't feel well	Δεν αισθάνομαι καλά	*den esthanome kala*
I have...	Έχω...	*ekho...*
- a cold	- κρύωμα	*- krioma*
- diarrhoea	- διάρροια	*- thiaria*
- a rash	- ένα εξάνθημα	*- ena eksanthima*
- a temperature	- πυρετό	*- pireto*
I have a lump here	Παρατήρησα ένα εξόγκωμα εδώ	*paratirisa ena eksogoma etho*
Can I have the morning-after pill?	Θα μπορούσα να έχω το χάπι της επόμενης μέρας;	*tha boroosa na ekho to khapee tees epomenis meras?*
It hurts here	Πονάει εδώ	*ponai etho*
It hurts a lot/a little	Πονάει πολύ/λίγο	*ponai polee/leego*
How much will it cost?	Πόσο θα κοστίσει;	*poso tha kostisi?*
I have insurance	Έχω ασφάλεια	*ekho asfalia*

Dentist

I need a dentist	Χρειάζομαι έναν οδοντίατρο	*khriazome enan othodiatro*
I have tooth ache	Έχω πονόδοντο	*ekho ponothodo*
My gums are swollen	Τα ούλα μου είναι πρησμένα	*ta ula mou ine prizmena*
This filling has fallen out	Μου χάλασε ένα σφράγισμα	*moo chalase ena sfrayizma*
I have an abscess	Έχω ένα απόστημα	*ekho ena aposteema*
I've broken a tooth	Μου έσπασε ένα δόντι	*moo espase ena thodi*

Are you going to take it out?	Θα το βγάλετε;	*tha to vghalete?*
Can you fix it temporarily?	Μπορείτε να το διορθώσετε προσωρινά;	*borite na to dhee-orthosete prosorina?*

Crime

I want to report a theft	Θέλω να δηλώσω μία κλοπή	*thelo na dheeloso meea klopee*
Someone has stolen my...	Κάποιος έχει κλέψει...	*kapios ekhee klepsee...*
- bags	- τις βαλίτσες μου	*- tis valitses mu*
- car	- το αυτοκίνητό μου	*- to aftokeeneto mu*
- credit cards	- τις πιστωτικές κάρτες μου	*- tis pistotikes kartes mu*
- money	- τα χρήματά μου	*- ta khrimata mu*
- passport	- το διαβατήριό μου	*- to thiavatirio mu*
I've been attacked	Μου επιτέθηκαν	*moo epitetheekan*

Mob mentality
Strikes and demonstrations frequently choke central Athens. Avoid getting swept up in these marches, which sometimes end with a rain of Molotov cocktails on the American Embassy.

Lost property

I've lost my...	Έχω χάσει...	*echo chasee...*
- car keys	- τα κλειδιά του αυτοκινήτου μου	*- ta kleedhya too aftokeeneetoo moo*
- driving licence	- την άδεια οδήγησης	*- teen adheea odheeyeesees*
- handbag	- την τσάντα μου	*- teen tsanda moo*
- flight tickets	- τα εισιτήριά μου	*- ta eeseeteereea moo*

It happened...	Συνέβη...	*seenevee...*
- this morning	- σήμερα το πρωί	- *simera to pro-ee*
- today	- σήμερα	- *simera*
- in the hotel	- στο ξενοδοχείο	- *sto ksenothohio*
I left it in the taxi	Το ξέχασα στο ταξί	*to ksechasa sto taksee*

Breakdowns

I've had...	Συνέβη...	*seenevee...*
- an accident	- ένα ατύχημα	- *ena atihima*
- a breakdown	- μία βλάβη	- *meea vlavi*
- a puncture	- ένα κλατάρισμα	- *ena klatareesma*

My battery is flat	Η μπαταρία μου είναι άδεια	*ee batareea mou ine adeia*
I don't have a spare tyre	Δεν έχω ρεζέρβα	*dhen ekho rezerva*
I've run out of petrol	Μου τελείωσε η βενζίνη	*mu teliose i venzinee*
My car doesn't start	Το αυτοκίνητο δεν παίρνει μπρος	*to aftokinito then pernee bros*

Can you repair it?	Μπορείτε να το επισκευάσετε;	*boreete na to episkevasete?*
How long will it take?	Πόση ώρα θα σας πάρει;	*posee ora tha sas paree?*
I have breakdown cover	Έχω ασφάλεια	*ekho asfalia*

Problems with the authorities

I'm sorry, I didn't realise...	Συγγνώμη. Δεν κατάλαβα...	*sighnomi. then katalava...*
- I was driving so fast	- ότι έτρεχα τόσο γρήγορα	- *oti etrekha toso ghreeghora*
- I went over the red lights	- ότι πέρασα με κόκκινο	- *oti perasa me kokeeno*
- it was against the law	- ότι ήταν παράνομο	- *oti eetan paranomo*

Here are my documents	Αυτά είναι τα χαρτιά μου	*afta ine ta khartia mu*
I'm innocent	Είμαι αθώος/α *m/f*	*ime atho-os/a*

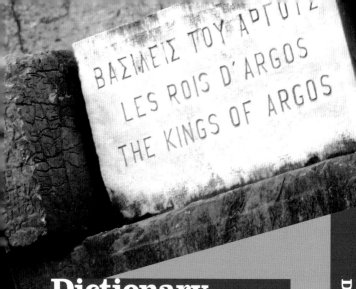

ΒΑΣΜΕΙΣ ΤΟΥ ΑΡΓΟΥΣ

LES ROIS D'ARGOS

THE KINGS OF ARGOS

Dictionary

There are three genders in Greek:
masculine, feminine and neuter. In this
chapter, nouns are given with their
articles. If individual nouns can be
either masculine or feminine, such as
'doctor', they are displayed with both
options. Adjectives agree with nouns
in gender, case and number and they
are placed in front of nouns. We list
them with their masculine, feminine
and neuter endings.

Mastering just a few Greek words and
phrases will open doors, especially in
small mountain villages but also in
bigger resorts. And if all else fails,
you can always point to the relevant
terms on the following pages.

English-Greek dictionary

A

a(n)	ένας/μία/ένα *m/f/n*	*enas/mia/ena*
about (concerning)	σχετικά με	*shetika me*
accident	ατύχημα, το	*atihima*
accommodation	κατάλυμα, το	*katalima*
A&E	επείγοντα, τα	*epeeghonda*
aeroplane	αεροπλάνο, το	*aeroplano*
again	πάλι	*pali*
ago	πριν	*prin*
AIDS	AIDS, το	*eids*
airmail	αεροπορικό ταχυδρομείο, το	*aeroporiko tahithomio*
airport	αεροδρόμιο, το	*aerothromio*
alarm	ξυπνητήρι, το	*ksipnitiri*
all	όλοι	*oli*
all right	εντάξει	*endahksi*
allergy	αλλεργία, η	*aleryia*
ambulance	ασθενοφόρο, το	*asthenoforo*
America	Αμερική, η	*ameriki*
American (thing)	αμερικάνικος/ αμερικάνικη *adj m/f*	*amerikanikos/ amerikaniki*
American (person)	αμερικάνος/αμερικανίδα *noun m/f*	*amerikanos/amerikanida*
and	και	*ke*

another	**ένας άλλος/μία άλλη/ένα άλλο** *m/f/n*	*enas alos/ mia alee/ena alo*

Order another beer with this phrase: "alli mia mpira parakalo" (*alee mia beera, parakalo*).

to answer	απαντώ	*apando*
any	καθόλου	*katholu*
apartment	διαμέρισμα, το	*thiamerizma*
appointment	ραντεβού, το	*radevu*
April	Απρίλιος, ο	*aprilios*
area	περιοχή, η	*periohi*
area code	ταχυδρομικός κωδικός, ο	*tahithromikos kothikos*
around	γύρω	*yiro*
to arrange	διευθετώ	*thieftheto*
arrivals	αφίξεις, οι	*afiksis*
art	τέχνη, η	*tehni*
to ask	ρωτάω	*rotao*
aspirin	ασπιρίνη, η	*aspirini*
at	σε	*se*
August	Αύγουστος, ο	*avghustos*
Australia	Αυστραλία, η	*afstralia*
Australian (thing)	αυστραλέζικος/ αυστραλέζικη *adj m/f*	*afstralezikos/ afstraleziki*
Australian (person)	Αυστραλός/Αυστραλέζα *noun m/f*	*afstralos/ afstraleza*
available	διαθέσιμος/η/ο *m/f/n*	*thiathesim-os/i/o*
away	μακριά	*makria*

B

baby	μωρό, το	*moro*
baggage	αποσκευές, οι	*aposkeves*
bar (pub)	μπαρ, το	*bar*
bath	μπάνιο, το	*banio*
bathing cap	σκούφος μπάνιου, ο	*skoofos baniu*
to be	είμαι	*ime*
beach	παραλία, η	*paralia*
because	διότι	*thioti*
best	ο καλύτερος/η καλύτερη/το καλύτερο *m/f/n*	*o kaliteros/ i kaliteri/ to kalitero*
better	καλύτερος/η/ο *m/f/n*	*kaliter-os/i/o*
between	ανάμεσα	*anamesa*
bicycle	ποδήλατο, το	*pothilato*
big	μεγάλος/η/ο *m/f/n*	*meghal-os/i/o*
bill	λογαριασμός, ο	*loghariazmos*
bit (a)	λίγο	*ligho*
boarding card	δελτίο επιβιβάσεως, το	*dhelteeo epivivaseos*
book	βιβλίο, το	*vivlio*
to book	κάνω κράτηση	*kano kratisi*
booking	κράτηση, η	*kratisi*
box office	ταμείο, το	*tamio*
boy	αγόρι, το	*aghori*
brother	αδελφός, ο	*adhelfos*
bureau de change	ξένο συνάλλαγμα, το	*kseno sinalaghma*
to burn	καίω	*keo*
bus	λεωφορείο, το	*leoforio*
business	δουλειά, η	*dhoolya*
business class	μπίζνες κλας, η	*biznes klas*
but	αλλά	*ala*
to buy	αγοράζω	*aghorazo*
by (beside)	δίπλα	*theepla*
by (by air, car, etc)	με	*me*
by (via)	με	*me*

C

| café | καφετερία, η | *kafeteria* |

A Greek Nescafé salesman invented frappé in 1957. He prepared instant coffee like a children's chocolate drink.

calculator	κομπιουτεράκι, το	*kombiuteraki*
to call	τηλεφωνώ	*tilefono*
camera	φωτογραφική μηχανή, η	*fotoghrafiki meekhani*
can (to be able)	μπορώ	*boro*
to cancel	ακυρώνω	*akeerono*
car	αυτοκίνητο, το	*aftokeeneeto*
carton (cigarettes)	πακέτο, το	*paketo*
cash	μετρητά, τα	*metrita*
cashpoint	μηχάνημα ανάληψης χρημάτων (ΑΤΜ), το	*mihanima analipsis chrimaton (ey tee em)*
casino	καζίνο, το	*kazeeno*
cathedral	μητρόπολη, η	*mitropoli*
CD	CD, το	*see dee*

centre	κέντρο, το	*kentro*
to change	αλλάζω	*alazo*
charge	τιμή, η	*teemi*
to charge	χρεώνω	*khreono*
cheap	φτηνός/ή/ό *m/f/n*	*fteen-os/i/o*
to check in (airport)	παραδίδω τις αποσκευές μου και παίρνω κάρτα επιβίβασης	*paratheetho tis aposkeves mu ke perno karta epivivasis*
to check in (hotel)	καταλύω (σε ξενοδοχείο)	*kataleeo (se ksenothoheeo)*
cheque	επιταγή, η	*epitayee*
children	παιδιά, τα	*pethia*
cigar	πούρο, το	*pooro*
cigarette	τσιγάρο, το	*tseegharo*

cinema	**κινηματογράφος, ο**	***keeneematoghrafos***

Athens is home to around 100 outdoor theatres, a tradition
that traces back to the 1916 projections in Syntagma Square.

city	πόλη, η	*poli*
to close	κλείνω	*kleeno*
close by	κοντινός/ή/ό *m/f/n*	*kondeen-os/i/o*
closed	κλειστός/ή/ό *m/f/n*	*kleest-os/i/o*
clothes	ρούχα, τα	*rookha*
club	κλαμπ, το	*klab*
coast	ακτή, η	*aktee*
cold	κρύος/α/ο *m/f/n*	*kree-os/a/o*
colour	χρώμα, το	*khroma*
to complain	παραπονούμαι	*paraponoome*
complaint	παράπονο, το	*parapono*
to confirm	επιβεβαιώνω	*epeeveveono*
confirmation	επιβεβαίωση, η	*epeeveveosi*
congratulations!	συγχαρητήρια, τα	*seenkhareeteereea*
consulate	προξενείο, το	*prokseneeo*
to contact	επικοινωνώ με	*epeekeenono me*
contagious	μεταδοτικός/ή/ό *m/f/n*	*metathotik-os/i/o*
cool	δροσερός/ή/ό *m/f/n*	*dhroser-os/i/o*
cost	κόστος, το	*kostos*
to cost	κοστίζει	*kosteezee*
cot	παιδικό κρεβάτι, το	*pethiko krevati*
country	χώρα, η	*khora*
countryside	εξοχή, η	*eksokhi*
cream	κρέμα, η	*krema*
credit card	πιστωτική κάρτα, η	*pistotiki karta*
crime	έγκλημα, το	*engkleema*
currency	νόμισμα, το	*nomisma*
customer	πελάτης, ο	*pelatees*
customs	τελωνείο, το	*teloneeo*
cut	κόψιμο, το	*kopseemo*
to cut	κόβω	*kovo*
cycling	ποδηλασία, η	*podheelasia*

D

damage	ζημιά, η	*zimia*
date (calendar)	ημερομηνία, η	*imeromineea*

daughter	κόρη, η	_kori_
day	ημέρα, η	_imera_
December	Δεκέμβριος, ο	_thekemvrios_
to dehydrate	αφυδατώνομαι	_afeethatonome_
delay	καθυστέρηση, η	_katheesterisi_
to dial	τηλεφωνώ	_teelefono_
difficult	δύσκολος/η/ο _m/f/n_	_dheeskol-os/i/o_
dining room	τραπεζαρία, η	_trapezareea_
directions	οδηγίες, οι	_odhighee-es_
dirty	βρώμικος/η/ο _m/f/n_	_vromeek-os/i/o_
disabled	άτομο με αναπηρία, το	_atomo me anapeereea_

disco   ντισκοτέκ, η   **_deeskotek_**
The pursuit of pleasure is important to Greeks. Hipsters often dance from midnight until breakfast time.

discount	έκπτωση, η	_ekptosee_
disinfectant	απολυμαντικό, το	_apoleemandeeko_
to disturb	διαταράσσω	_thiatarasso_
doctor	γιατρός, ο/η	_yiatros, o/i_
double	διπλός/ή/ό _m/f/n_	_thipl-os/i/o_
down	κάτω	_kato_
to drive	οδηγώ	_odhigho_
driver	οδηγός, ο/η	_odhighos, o/i_
driving licence	άδεια οδήγησης, η	_adheea odhiyisis_
drug	ναρκωτικό, το	_narkoteeko_
to dry clean	στεγνοκαθαρίζω	_steghnokathareezo_
dry-cleaner's	καθαριστήριο, το	_kathareesteereeo_
during	κατά τη διάρκεια	_kata tee dheearkeea_
duty (tax)	δασμός, ο	_thasmos_

E

| early | νωρίς | _norees_ |
| to eat | τρώω | _tro-o_ |

e-mail   ημέιλ/e-mail, το   **_imeil_**
Online access is excellent. One reliable chain is easyInternetcafé, owned by Greek easyJet entrepreneur Stelios.

embassy	πρεσβεία, η	_presveea_
emergency	επείγουσα ανάγκη, η	_epeeghusa anaghi_
England	Αγγλία, η	_angglia_
English (thing)	αγγλικός/ή/ό _adj m/f/n_	_angglikos/i/o_
English (person)	Άγγλος/Αγγλίδα _noun m/f_	_angglos/angglida_
English (language)	αγγλικά _(language)_	_angglika_
to enjoy	διασκεδάζω	_dheeaskedhazo_
enough	αρκετά	_arketa_
error	λάθος, το	_lathos_
exactly	ακριβώς	_akrivos_
exchange rate	τιμή συναλλάγματος, η	_timi seenalaghmatos_
exhibition	έκθεση, η	_ekthesee_
to export	εξάγω	_eksagho_
express (delivery)	κατεπείγον, το	_katepeeghon_
express (train)	ταχεία, η	_takheea_

F

facilities	εγκαταστάσεις, οι	*eghatastasees*
far	μακριά	*makreea*
father	πατέρας, ο	*pateras*
favourite	αγαπημένος/η/ο *m/f/n*	*aghapeemen-os/i/o*
to fax	στέλνω φαξ	*stelno faks*
February	Φεβρουάριος, ο	*fevruarios*
filling (station)	πρατήριο βενζίνης, το	*pratirio venzeenis*
fill her up (petrol)	γεμίστε το	*yemeeste to*
film (camera)	φιλμ, το	*feelm*

film (cinema)	**ταινία, η**	***teneea***

The quintessential Athenian film is 1960's *Never on Sunday*, starring Melina Mercouri as a heart-of-gold prostitute.

to finish	τελειώνω	*teleeono*
fire	φωτιά, η	*fotya*
first aid	πρώτες βοήθειες, οι	*protes voeetheeys*
fitting room	δοκιμαστήριο, το	*dhokimastirio*
flight	πτήση, η	*ptisi*
flu	γρίπη, η	*ghreepi*
food poisoning	τροφική δηλητηρίαση, η	*trofeeki dhilitireeasee*
football	ποδόσφαιρο, το	*podhosfero*
for	για	*ya*
form (document)	έντυπο, το	*enteepo*
free (money)	δωρεάν, ο/η/το *m/f/n*	*dhorean, o/ee/to*
free (vacant)	ελεύθερος/η/ο *m/f/n*	*eleftheros/i/o*
friend (male)	φίλος, ο *m*	*filos*
friend (female)	φίλη, η *f*	*fili*
from	από	*apo*

G

gallery	πινακοθήκη, η	*peenakotheekee*
garage	γκαράζ, το	*garaz*
gas	γκάζι, το	*gazee*
gents	τουαλέτα ανδρών, η	*tualeta andhron*
to get	παίρνω	*perno*
girl	κορίτσι, το	*koreetsee*
to give	δίνω	*dheeno*
to go	πηγαίνω	*peeyeno*
golf	γκολφ, το	*golf*
golf course	γήπεδο του γκολφ, το	*yeepedho too golf*
good	καλός/ή/ό *m/f/n*	*kal-os/i/o*
Greece	Ελλάδα	*eladha*
Greek (person)	Έλληνας/Ελληνίδα *noun m/f*	*elinas/elinidha*
Greek (thing)	ελληνικός/ή/ό *adj m/f/n*	*elinikos/i/o*
Greek (language)	ελληνικά *(language)*	*elinika*
group	ομάδα, η	*omadha*
guarantee	εγγύηση, η	*engeeyeesee*
guide	ξεναγός, το	*ksenaghos*

H

hair	μαλλιά, τα	*malya*
hairdresser's	κομμωτήριο, το	*komoteerio*

half	μισό, το	meeso
to have	έχω	ekho
heat	ζέστη, η	zestee
help!	βοήθεια!	voithia!
to help	βοηθώ	voitho
here	εδώ	etho
to hire	νοικιάζω	neekiazo
holiday	διακοπές, οι	dheeakopes
homosexual	ομοφυλόφιλος/η/o m/f/n	omofeelofil-os/i/o
horse riding	ιππασία, η	ipasia
hospital	νοσοκομείο, το	nosokomio
hot	ζεστός/ή/ό m/f/n	zest-os/i/o
how?	πώς;	pos?
how big?	πόσο μεγάλος/η/o; m/f/n	poso meghalos/i/o?
how far?	πόσο μακριά;	poso makreea?
how long? (time)	πόση ώρα;	posee ora?
how long? (length)	τι μήκος έχει;	Tee meekos echee?
how much? (money)	πόσο κοστίζει;	poso kosteezee?
to be hungry	πεινώ	peeno
hurry up!	κάνε γρήγορα	kane ghrighora
to hurt	πονώ	pono
husband	σύζυγος, ο	sizighos

I

identity card	ταυτότητα, η	taftoteeta
ill (m)	άρρωστος, ο m	arostos
ill (f)	άρρωστη, η f	arosti
ill (n)	άρρωστο, το n	arosto
immediately	αμέσως	amesos
to import	εισάγω	isagho
important	σπουδαίος/α/o m/f/n	spoodh-eos/a/o
in	μέσα	mesa
information	πληροφορίες, οι	pliroforee-es
inside	στο εσωτερικό	sto esotereeko
insurance	ασφάλεια, η	asfalia
interesting (m)	ενδιαφέρων, ο m	endheeaferon
interesting (f)	ενδιαφέρουσα, η f	endheeaferusa
interesting (n)	ενδιαφέρον, το n	endheeaferon
international (m/f)	διεθνής, ο/η m/f	dhiethnees, o/i

international(n)	διεθνές, το n	**dhiethnes**

Many Greeks live abroad but remain passionate about their homeland, reflected in the *diaspora* art.

Ireland	Ιρλανδία, η	eerlandheea
Irish (person)	Ιρλανδός/Ιρλανδή noun m/f	eerlandhos/eerlandhee
Irish (thing)	ιρλανδικός/ή/ό adj m/f/n	eerlandikos/i/o
Irish (language)	ιρλανδικά (language)	eerlandeeka
island	νησί, το	neesee
itinerary	δρομολόγιο, το	dromoloyeeo

J

January	Ιανουάριος, ο	ianuarios
jellyfish	τσούχτρα, η	tsookhtra

jet ski	τζετ σκι, το	jetski
journey	ταξίδι, το	takseedhee
July	Ιούλιος, ο	iulios
junction	διασταύρωση, η	dheeastavrosee
June	Ιούνιος, ο	iunios
just (only)	μόνο	mono

K

to keep	κρατώ	krato
key	κλειδί, το	kleedhee
keyring	μπρελόκ, το	brelok
keyboard	πληκτρολόγιο, το	pleektrologhio
to kill	σκοτώνω	skotono
kind (nice)	ευγενικός/ή/ό m/f/n	efgheneek-os/i/o
kind (sort)	είδος	eedhos

| **kiosk** | περίπτερο, το | **pereeptero** |

Stands sell newspapers, drinks, aspirin, stamps and other essentials – and they're open later than shops.

kiss	φιλί, το	feeli
to kiss	φιλώ	feelo
to know (knowledge)	ξέρω	ksero
to know (person)	γνωρίζω	gnoreezo

L

ladies (toilets)	τουαλέτα γυναικών, η	tualeta yeenekon
lady	κυρία, η	keereea
language	γλώσσα, η	ghlosa
last	τελευταίος/α/ο m/f/n	telefte-os/a/o
late (delayed)	καθυστερημένος/η/ο m/f/n	katheesterimen-os/i/o
late (time)	αργά	argha
launderette	πλυντήριο, το	pleendeereeo
lawyer	δικηγόρος, ο	dheekighoros
to leave	φεύγω	fevgho
left	αριστερά	areestera
less	λιγότερος/η/ο m/f/n	leeghoter-os/i/o
letter	γράμμα	ghrama
library	βιβλιοθήκη, η	veevleeotheekee
life jacket	σωσίβιο, το	soseeveeo
lifeguard	ναυαγοσώστης, ο	navaghosostees
lift	ασανσέρ, το	asanser
to like	μου αρέσει	moo aresee
to listen to	ακούω	akuo
little (a little)	λίγο	leegho
local	τοπικός/ή/ό m/f/n	topeek-os/i/o
to look	κοιτάζω	keetazo
to lose	χάνω	hano
lost property	απωλεσθέντα, τα	apolesthenda
luggage	αποσκευές, οι	aposkeves

M

madam	κυρία, η	keereea
mail	ταχυδρομείο, το	takheedhromeeo
main	κυρίως	keereeos

to make	κάνω	*kano*
man	άνδρας, ο	*andras*
manager	διευθυντής, ο	*thieftheendhees*
many	πολλοί/ές/ά *m/f/n*	*polee-es-a*
map (city)	χάρτης πόλης, ο	*khartees polis*
map (road)	χάρτης δρόμου, ο	*khartees dhromoo*
March	Μάρτιος, ο	*martios*
market	αγορά, η	*aghora*
married	παντρεμένος/η/ο *m/f/n*	*padremen-os/i/o*
May	Μάιος, ο	*ma-ee-os*
mechanic	μηχανικός, ο	*meekhaneekos*
to meet	συναντώ	*seenando*
meeting	συνάντηση, η	*seenandisi*
message	μήνυμα, το	*meeneema*
midday	μεσημέρι, το	*mesimeri*
midnight	μεσάνυχτα, τα	*mesaneekhta*
minimum	ελάχιστος/η/ο *m/f/n*	*elakheest-os/i/o*
minute	λεπτό, το	*lepto*
to miss (a person)	μου λείπει	*moo leepee*
to miss (a train)	χάνω	*khano*
missing	λείπει	*leepee*
mobile phone	κινητό τηλέφωνο, το	*keeneeto tilefono*
moment	στιγμή, η	*steegmee*
money	χρήματα, τα	*khrimata*
more	περισσότερο	*pereesotero*
mosquito	κουνούπι, το	*koonoopee*
most	ο περισσότερος/η περισσότερη/το περισσότερο *m/f/n*	*o pereesoteros/i pereesoteri/to pereesotero*
mother	μητέρα, η	*meetera*
much	πολύ	*polee*
museum	μουσείο, το	*mooseeo*

| **musical** | **μιούζικαλ, το** | *miuzeekal* |

Mikis Theodorakis composed the *Zorba the Greek* soundtrack, fusing **laika** (ballads), **rembetika** (blues) and classical motifs.

| must | πρέπει | *prepee* |
| my | δικό μου | *deeko mu* |

N

name	όνομα, το	*onoma*
nationality	υπηκοότητα, η	*epeeko-oteeta*
near	κοντά	*konda*
necessary	απαραίτητος/η/ο *m/f/n*	*apareteet-os/i/o*
to need	χρειάζομαι	*khriazome*
never	ποτέ	*pote*
new	καινούριος/α/ο *m/f/n*	*kenoory-os/a/o*
news	ειδήσεις	*eedheesees*

| **newspaper** | **εφημερίδα, η** | *efeemereedha* |

The Athens News is the weekly English-language newspaper, but *Time Out Athens* has entertainment listings.

next	επόμενος/η/ο *m/f/n*	*epomen-os/i/o*
next to	δίπλα σε	*dheepla se*
nice (people)	καλός/ή/ό *m/f/n*	*kal-os/i/o*
nice (things)	ωραίος/α/ο *m/f/n*	*ore-os/a/o*
night	νύχτα, η	*neekhta*
nightclub	νυχτερινό κέντρο, το	*neekhtereeno kendro*
north	βορράς, ο	*voras*
note (money)	χαρτονόμισμα, το	*khartonomeesma*
nothing	τίποτα	*teepota*
November	Νοέμβριος, ο	*noemvrios*
now	τώρα	*tora*
nudist beach	παραλία γυμνιστών, η	*paraleea yeemneeston*
number	αριθμός, ο	*areethmos*

O

object	αντικείμενο, το	*adhekeemeno*
October	Οκτώβριος, ο	*oktovrios*
off (food)	είναι χαλασμένο	*ine khalasmeno*
off (switched)	σβηστός/ή/ό *m/f/n*	*sveest-os/i/o*
office	γραφείο, το	*ghrafeeo*

OK	**ενταξει**	***endaksee***

'OK' – **entaksei** – is a common phrase. **Eimai entaksei** (*ime endaksee*) means 'I'm all right'.

on	πάνω	*pano*
only	μόνο	*mono*
open	ανοικτός/ή/ό *m/f/n*	*aneekt-os/i/o*
to open	ανοίγω	*aneegho*
operator	τηλεφων-ητής/ήτρια *m/f*	*tilefon-itis/itria*
opposite (place)	απέναντι	*apenandee*
optician's	οπτικός, ο/η	*optikos, o/i*
or	ή	*ee*
to order	παραγγέλλω	*parangelo*
other	άλλος/η/ο *m/f/n*	*alos/ali/alo*
out of order	εκτός λειτουργίας	*ektos leetoorgheeas*
outdoor	εξωτερικός χώρος	*eksotereekos horos*
outside	έξω	*ekso*
overnight	για μια νύχτα	*yia meea neechta*
owner (m)	ιδιοκτήτης, ο *m*	*eedheeokteetees*
owner (f)	ιδιοκτήτρια, η *f*	*eedheeokteetria*
oxygen	οξυγόνο, το	*okseeghono*

P

painkiller	παυσίπονο, το	*pafseepono*
pair	ζευγάρι, το	*zevgharee*
parents	γονείς, οι	*ghonees*
park	πάρκο, το	*parko*
to park	παρκάρω	*parkaro*
parking	στάθμευση, η	*stathmefsi*
party	πάρτυ, το	*party*
passport	διαβατήριο, το	*thiavatirio*
to pay	πληρώνω	*plirono*
people	άνθρωποι, οι	*anthropee*
person	άτομο, το	*atomo*

phone	τηλέφωνο, το	*tilefono*
to phone	τηλεφωνώ	*tilefono*
photo	φωτογραφία, η	*fotoghrafeea*
phrase book	λεξικό χρήσιμων φράσεων, το	*leksiko chrisimon fraseon*
place	τόπος, ο	*topos*
platform	αποβάθρα, η	*apovathra*
police	αστυνομία, η	*astinomia*
port (drink)	πορτό, το	*porto*
port (sea)	λιμάνι, το	*leemanee*
possible	πιθανό	*peethano*
post	ταχυδρομώ	*takheedhromo*
post office	ταχυδρομείο, το	*takheedhromeeo*
to prefer	προτιμώ	*proteemo*

| **prescription** | **συνταγή, η** | ***seendayee*** |

Some UK over-the-counter medicines – like Nurofen Plus – require a prescription here: carry a doctor's letter.

price	τιμή, η	*teemi*
private	ιδιωτικός/ή/ό *m/f/n*	*eedheeoteek-os/i/o*
probably	πιθανώς	*peethanos*
problem	πρόβλημα, το	*provlima*
pub	παμπ, η	*pab*
public transport	δημόσια μέσα μεταφοράς, τα	*dheemoseea mesa metaforas*
to put	βάζω	*vazo*

Q

quality	ποιότητα, η	*peeoteeta*
quantity	ποσότητα, η	*posoteeta*
quarter	τέταρτο, το	*tetarto*
query	ρωτώ	*roto*
question	ερώτηση, η	*eroteesee*
queue	ουρά, η	*oora*
quick	γρήγορος/η/ο *m/f/n*	*ghreeghor-os/i/o*
quickly	γρήγορα	*ghreeghora*
quiet	ήσυχος/η/ο *m/f/n*	*isikh-os/i/o*
quite	αρκετά	*arketa*

R

radio	ραδιόφωνο, το	*radheeofono*
railway	σιδηρόδρομος, ο	*seedheerodhromos*
rain	βροχή, η	*vrokhee*
rape	βιασμός, ο	*veeasmos*
razor blade	ξυραφάκι, το	*kseerafakee*
ready	έτοιμος/η/ο *m/f/n*	*eteem-os/i/o*
receipt	απόδειξη, η	*apodheeksee*
to receive	λαμβάνω	*lamvano*
reception	υποδοχή, η	*ipothokhi*
receptionist	υπάλληλος υποδοχής, ο/η	*ipalilos ipothokhis, o/i*
to recommend	συνιστώ	*seeneesto*
reduction	έκπτωση, η	*ekptosee*
refund	επιστροφή χρημάτων, η	*epeestrofee khrimaton*
to refuse	αρνούμαι	*arnoomai*

to relax	ξεκουράζομαι	ksekoorazome
rent	νοίκι, το	neekee
to rent	νοικιάζω	neekyazo
to request	ζητάω	zeetao
reservation	κράτηση, η	kratisi
to reserve	κάνω κράτηση	kano kratisi
retired	συνταξιούχος, ο/η	seendakseeookhos, o/i
to ride (horse)	ιππεύω	eepevo
to ride (bicycle)	κάνω ποδήλατο	kano podheelato
right	δεξιά	dheksya
to be right	έχω δίκιο	eho deekyo
to ring (a person)	τηλεφωνώ	tilefono
road	δρόμος, ο	dhromos
to rob	ληστεύω	leestevo
room	δωμάτιο, το	thomatio
route	διαδρομή, η	deeadromee
rude (m/f)	αγενής m/f	aghenees
rude (n)	αγενές n	aghenes
ruins	ερείπια, τα	ereepya
to run	τρέχω	trekho

S

safe	χρηματοκιβώτιο, το	khrimatokivotio
Scotland	Σκωτία, η	skoteea
Scottish (person)	Σκωτσέζος/α noun m/f	skotsezos/a
Scottish (thing)	σκωτσέζικος/η/ο adj m/f/n	skotsezikos/i/o
sea	θάλασσα, η	thalasa
seat	θέση, η	thesee
seat belt	ζώνη ασφαλείας, η	zoni asfalias
sedative	ηρεμιστικό, το	eeremisteeko
see you later	τα λέμε αργότερα	ta leme arghotera
self-service	σελφ σέρβις, το	self service
to sell	πουλώ	poolo
to send	στέλνω	stelno
sensible	φρόνιμος/η/ο m/f/n	fronim-os/i/o
September	Σεπτέμβριος, ο	septemvrios
to serve	σερβίρω	serveero
service	εξυπηρέτηση, η	ekseepeereteesee
shop	ψωνίζω	psoneezo
shopping	ψώνια, τα	psonia

shopping centre	εμπορικό κέντρο, το	emporiko kendro

Athens' DESTE Centre mixes art, multimedia, events and shopping in a renovated paper warehouse (www.deste.gr).

short	κοντός/ή/ό m/f/n	kond-os/i/o
show	παράσταση, η	parastasee
to show	δείχνω	dheekhno
shut	κλειστός/ή/ό m/f/n	kleest-os/i/o
sign	πινακίδα, η	peenakeedha
to sign	υπογράφω	eepoghrafo
signature	υπογραφή, η	eepoghrafee
since	από τότε που	apo tote pu
sir	κύριος, ο	kirios
sister	αδελφή, η	adhelfee

ski	σκι, το	ski
to sleep	κοιμάμαι	keemame
sleeping pill	υπνωτικό χάπι, το	eepnoteeko khapee
slow	αργά	argha
small	μικρός/ή/ό m/f/n	meekr-os/i/o
to smoke	καπνίζω	kapneezo
soft	μαλακός/ή/ό m/f/n	malak-os/i/o
some	μερικοί/ές/ά m/f/n	mereekee/es/a
something	κάτι	katee
son	γιος, ο	yios
soon	σύντομα	seendoma
south	νότος, ο	notos
South Africa	Νότιος Αφρική, η	noteeos afriki
South African (person)	Νοτιοαφρικάνος/α noun m/f	noteeoafrikanos/a
South African (thing)	νοτιοαφρικανικός/ή/ό adj m/f/n	noteeoafrikanikos/i/o
to spell	συλλαβίζω	seelaveezo
sport	σπορ, το	spor
stadium	στάδιο, το	stadheeo
staff	προσωπικό, το	prosopiko
stamp	γραμματόσημο, το	ghramatoseemo
to start	αρχίζω	arkheezo
to start (car)	βάζω μπρος	vazo mbros
station	σταθμός, ο	stathmos
sterling pound	αγγλική λίρα, η	angliki lira
to stop	σταματώ	stamato
straight	ευθεία, η	eftheea
street	δρόμος, ο	dhromos
stress	άγχος, το	anghos
suddenly	ξαφνικά	ksafneeka
suitcase	βαλίτσα, η	valeetsa
sun	ήλιος, ο	eelios
sunglasses	γυαλιά ηλίου, τα	yalya eeleeoo
surname	επώνυμο, το	eponeemo
swimming pool	πισίνα, η	pisina
symptom	σύμπτωμα, το	seemptoma

T

table	τραπέζι, το	trapezee
to take	παίρνω	perno
tall	ψηλός/ή/ό m/f/n	psel-os/i/o
tampons	ταμπόν, το	tambon
tax	φόρος, ο	foros
tax free	αφορολόγητος/η/ο m/f/n	aforoloyeet-os/i/o
taxi	ταξί, το	taksi
taxi rank	πιάτσα ταξί, η	pyatsa taksee
telephone	τηλέφωνο, το	tilefono
telephone box	τηλεφωνικός θάλαμος, ο	teelefoneekos thalamos
television	τηλεόραση, η	teeleorasee
tennis	τένις, το	tenees
tennis court	γήπεδο του τένις, το	yeepedho too tenees
terrace	ταράτσα, η	taratsa
to text	στέλνω sms	stelno sms
that	εκείνος/η/ο m/f/n	ekeen-os/i/o

theft	κλοπή, η	*klopee*
then	τότε	*tote*
there	εκεί	*ekee*
thing	πράγμα, το	*praghma*
to think	σκέφτομαι	*skeftomai*
thirsty	διψάω	*dheepsao*
this	αυτός/ή/ό *m/f/n*	*aft-os/i/o*
through	διαμέσου	*dheeamesoo*
ticket (bus)	εισιτήριο, το	*eeseeteereeo*
ticket (cinema)	εισιτήριο, το	*eeseeteereeo*
ticket (parking)	κλήση, η	*kleesee*
ticket office	γραφείο έκδοσης εισητηρίων, το	*grafeeo ekdosis eeseeteereeon*
time	χρόνος, ο	*chronos*
time (clock)	ώρα, η	*ora*
timetable	δρομολόγιο, το	*dromoloyeeo*
tip (money)	φιλοδώρημα, το	*filodhoreema*
tired	κουρασμένος/η/ο *m/f/n*	*koorasmen-os/i/o*
to	σε	*se*
tobacco	καπνός, ο	*kapnos*
today	σήμερα	*seemera*
toilet	τουαλέτα, η	*tooaleta*
toiletries	είδη καλλωπισμού, τα	*eedi kalopeesmoo*
toll	διόδια, τα	*dheeodheea*
tomorrow	αύριο	*avreeo*
tonight	απόψε	*apopse*
too	επίσης	*epeesees*

| **tourist office** | **οργανισμός τουρισμού, ο** | *orghaneesmos toorismoo* |

Contact the Greek National Tourist Organisation at
2 Amerikis Street, Athens (210 331 0565; www.gnto.gr).

town	πόλη, η	*polee*
town hall	δημαρχείο, το	*dheemarkheeo*
train	τρένο, το	*treno*
tram	τραμ, το	*tram*
to translate	μεταφράζω	*metafrazo*
travel	ταξιδεύω	*takseedhevo*
travel agency	ταξιδιωτικό πρακτορείο, το	*takseedhyoteeko praktoreeo*
true	αληθινός/ή/ό *m/f/n*	*aleetheen-os/i/o*
typical	τυπικός/ή/ό *m/f/n*	*teepeek-os/i/o*

U

ugly	άσχημος/η/ο *m/f/n*	*askheem-os/i/o*
ulcer	έλκος, το	*elkos*
umbrella	ομπρέλα, η	*ombrela*
uncomfortable	άβολος/η/ο *m/f/n*	*avol-os/i/o*
unconscious	αναίσθητος/η/ο *m/f/n*	*anestheet-os/i/o*
under	κάτω από	*kato apo*
underground (tube)	μετρό, το	*metro*
to understand	καταλαβαίνω	*katalaveno*
underwear	εσώρουχα, τα	*esorookha*
unemployed	άνεργος/η/ο *m/f/n*	*anergh-os/i/o*

unpleasant	δυσάρεστος/η/ο *m/f/n*	*dees<u>a</u>rest-os/i/o*
up	επάνω	*ep<u>a</u>no*
upstairs	επάνω	*ep<u>a</u>no*
urgent	επείγον	*ep<u>ee</u>ghon*
to use	χρησιμοποιώ	*khreeseemop<u>yo</u>*
useful	χρήσιμος/η/ο *m/f/n*	*khr<u>ee</u>seem-os/i/o*
usually	συνήθως	*seen<u>ee</u>thos*

V

vacant	διαθέσιμος/η/ο *m/f/n*	*dheea<u>the</u>seem-os/i/o*
vacation	διακοπές, οι	*thiakop<u>es</u>*
vaccination	εμβολιασμός, ο	*emvoleeasm<u>os</u>*
valid	έγκυρος/η/ο *m/f/n*	*engkeer-os/i/o*
valuables	πολύτιμα αντικείμενα, τα	*poleeteema andeek<u>ee</u>mena*
value	αξία, η	*aks<u>ee</u>a*
VAT	ΦΠΑ, ο	*fee pee a*
vegetarian	χορτοφάγος, ο/η	*khorto<u>fa</u>ghos, o/i*
vehicle	όχημα, το	*<u>o</u>kheema*
very	πάρα	*<u>pa</u>ra*
visa	βίζα, η	*v<u>ee</u>sa*
visit	επίσκεψη, η	*ep<u>ee</u>skepsee*
to visit	επισκέπτομαι	*ep<u>ee</u>skeptomai*
vitamin	βιταμίνη, η	*veet<u>a</u>meenee*
to vomit	κάνω εμετό	*<u>ka</u>no emet<u>o</u>*

W

waiter/waitress	σερβιτόρος, ο /σερβιτόρα, η	*serveet<u>o</u>ros/ serveet<u>o</u>ra*
waiting room	αίθουσα αναμονής, η	*<u>e</u>thoosa anamon<u>ee</u>s*
Wales	Ουαλία, η	*ooal<u>ee</u>a*
to walk	περπατώ	*perpat<u>o</u>*
wallet	πορτοφόλι, το	*portof<u>o</u>lee*
to want	θέλω	*th<u>e</u>lo*
to wash	πλένω	*pl<u>e</u>no*
watch	ρολόι, το	*rol<u>o</u>ee*
to watch	βλέπω	*vl<u>e</u>po*
water	νερό, το	*ner<u>o</u>*
water sports	θαλάσσια σπορ, τα	*thal<u>a</u>seea spor*
way (manner)	τρόπος, ο	*tropos*
way (route)	δρόμος, ο	*dromos*
way in	είσοδος, η	*<u>ee</u>sodhos*
way out	έξοδος, η	*<u>e</u>ksodhos*
weather	καιρός, ο	*ker<u>os</u>*
web	διαδίκτυο, το	*thia<u>th</u>iktio*
website	ιστοσελίδα, η	*eestosel<u>ee</u>da*
week	εβδομάδα, η	*evthom<u>a</u>tha*
weekday	καθημερινή, η	*katheemereen<u>ee</u>*
weekend	Σαββατοκύριακο, το	*savato<u>ki</u>riako*
welcome	καλώς ήλθατε	*kalos <u>ee</u>lthate*
well (healthy)	υγιής *m/f* υγιές *n*	*eeyee<u>-ees</u>/eeyee<u>-es</u>*
Welsh (person)	Ουαλός/ή *noun m/f*	*ooal<u>os</u>/i*
Welsh (thing)	ουαλικός/ή/ό *adj m/f/n*	*ooalik-<u>os</u>/i/<u>o</u>*
Welsh (language)	ουαλικά *(language)*	*ooal<u>i</u>ka*
west	δύση, η	*dh<u>ee</u>see*

what?	τι;	*tee?*
wheelchair	αναπηρική καρέκλα, η	*anapirikee karekla*
when?	πότε;	*pote?*
where?	πού;	*pu?*
which?	ποιο;	*pio?*
while	ενώ	*eno*
who?	ποιος;	*pios?*
why?	γιατί;	*yiati?*
wife	σύζυγος, η	*sizighos*
to win	νικώ	*neeko*
with	με	*me*
without	χωρίς	*khorees*
woman	γυναίκα, η	*yeeneka*
wonderful	θαυμάσιος/α/ο *m/f/n*	*thavmasee-os/a/o*
word	λέξη, η	*leksee*
work	δουλειά, η	*dhoolya*
to work (machine)	λειτουργεί	*leetooryee*
to work (person)	δουλεύω	*dhoolevo*
world	κόσμος, ο	*kosmos*
worried	ανήσυχος/η/ο *m/f/n*	*aneeseekh-os/i/o*
worse	χειρότερος/η/ο *m/f/n*	*kheeroter-os/i/o*
to write	γράφω	*ghrafo*
wrong (mistaken)	κάνω λάθος	*kano lathos*

X

| xenophobe | ξενόφοβος/η/ο *m/f/n* | *ksenofov-os/i/o* |

| **xenophobia** | **ξενοφοβία** | ***ksenofoveea*** |

**The opposite of xenophobia is xenophilia. Generosity
towards guests remains a bedrock belief in Greece.**

x-ray	ακτινογραφία, η	*akteenoghrafeea*
to x-ray	βγάζω ακτινογραφία	*vghazo akteenoghrafeea*
x-rays	ακτίνες Χ, οι	*akteenes X*

Y

yacht	γιοτ, το	*yacht*
year	χρόνος, ο	*khronos*
yearly	ετήσιος/α/ο *m/f/n*	*eteesi-os/a/o*
yellow pages	Χρυσός Οδηγός, ο	*chreesos odheeghos*
yes	ναι	*ne*
yesterday	εχθές	*ekthes*
you (formal)	εσύ	*esee*
you (informal)	εσείς	*esees*
young	νέος/α/ο *m/f/n*	*ne-os/a/o*
your (formal)	δικός σου	*deekos su*
your (informal)	δικός σας	*deekos sas*
youth hostel	ξενώνας νεότητας, ο	*ksenonas neoteetas*

Z

zebra crossing	διάβαση πεζών, η	*theeavasi pezon*
zero	μηδέν, το	*mithen*
zip	φερμουάρ, το	*fermooar*
zone	ζώνη, η	*zonee*
zoo	ζωολογικός κήπος, ο	*zo-oloyeekos keepos*

Greek-English dictionary

A

άβολος/η/ο m/f/n	avol-os/i/o	uncomfortable
αγαπημένος/η/ο m/f/n	aghapeemen-os/i/o	favourite
Αγγλία, η	angg	England
αγγλικά (language)	angglika	English (language)
αγγλική λίρα, η	angliki lira	sterling pound
αγγλικός/ή/ό adj m/f/n	angglikos/i/o	English (thing)
Άγγλος/Αγγλίδα noun m/f	angglos/angglida	English (person)
αγενές n	aghenes	rude (n)
αγενής m/f	aghenees	rude (m/f)
αγορά, η	aghora	market
αγοράζω	aghorazo	to buy
αγόρι, το	aghori	boy
άγχος, το	anghos	stress
άδεια οδήγησης, η	adheea odhiyisis	driving licence
αδελφή, η	adhelfee	sister
αδελφός, ο	adhelfos	brother

αεροδρόμιο, το	aerothromio	airport

Athens built a sleek new airport, Eleftherios Venizelos, just before the 2004 Olympics.

αεροπλάνο, το	aeroplano	aeroplane
αεροπορικό ταχυδρομείο, το	aeroporiko tahithomio	airmail
AIDS, το	eids	AIDS
αίθουσα αναμονής, η	ethoosa anamonees	waiting room
ακόμα	akoma	yet
ακούω	akuo	to listen to
ακριβώς	akrivos	exactly
ακτή, η	aktee	coast
ακτίνες Χ, οι	akteenes x	x-rays
ακτινογραφία, η	akteenoghrafeea	x-ray
ακυρώνω	akeerono	to cancel
αληθινός/ή/ό m/f/n	aleetheen-os/i/o	true
αλλά	ala	but
αλλάζω	alazo	to change
αλλεργία, η	aleryia	allergy
άλλος/η/ο m/f/n	alos/ali/alo	other
αμερικάνικος/ αμερικάνικη adj m/f	amerikanikos/ amerikaniki	American (thing)
Αμερικάνος/ Αμερικανίδα noun m/f	amerikanos/ amerikanida	American (person)

Αμερική, η	ameriki	America

Some Greeks are highly critical of the US government, but welcome its citizens. Avoid political discussions, however.

αμέσως	amesos	immediately
αναίσθητος/η/ο m/f/n	anestheet-os/i/o	unconscious
ανάμεσα	anamesa	between
αναπηρική καρέκλα, η	anapirikee karekla	wheelchair

79

άνδρας, ο	andras	man
άνεργος/η/ο m/f/n	anergh-os/i/o	unemployed
ανήσυχος/η/ο m/f/n	aneeseekh-os/i/o	worried
άνθρωποι, οι	anthropee	people
ανοίγω	aneegho	to open
ανοικτός/ή/ό m/f/n	aneekt-os/i/o	open
αντικείμενο, το	adhekeemeno	object
αξία, η	akseea	value
απαντώ	apando	to answer
απαραίτητος/η/ο m/f/n	apareteet-os/i/o	necessary
απέναντι	apenandee	opposite (place)
από	apo	from
από τότε που	apo tote pu	since
αποβάθρα, η	apovathra	platform
απόδειξη, η	apodheeksee	receipt
απολυμαντικό, το	apoleemandeeko	disinfectant
αποσκευές, οι	aposkeves	luggage
απόψε	apopse	tonight
Απρίλιος, ο	aprilios	April
απωλεσθέντα, τα	apolesthenda	lost property
αργά	argha	late (time)
αργά	argha	slow
αριθμός, ο	areethmos	number
αριστερά	areestera	left
αρκετά	arketa	enough
αρκετά	arketa	quite
αρνούμαι	arnoomai	to refuse
άρρωστη, η f	arosti	ill (f)
άρρωστο, το n	arosto	ill (n)
άρρωστος, ο m	arostos	ill (m)
αρχίζω	arkheezo	to start
ασανσέρ, το	asanser	lift
ασθενοφόρο, το	asthenoforo	ambulance
ασπιρίνη, η	aspirini	aspirin
αστυνομία, η	astinomia	police
ασφάλεια, η	asfalia	insurance
άσχημος/η/ο m/f/n	askheem-os/i/o	ugly
άτομο με αναπηρία, το	atomo me anapeereea	disabled
άτομο, το	atomo	person
ατύχημα, το	atihima	accident
Αύγουστος, ο	avghustos	August
αύριο	avreeo	tomorrow
αυστραλέζικος/ αυστραλέζικη adj m/f	afstralezikos/ afstraleziki	Australian (thing)
Αυστραλία, η	afstralia	Australia
Αυστραλός/Αυστραλέζα noun m/f	afstralos/afstraleza	Australian (person)
αυτοκίνητο, το	aftokeeneeto	car
αυτός/ή/ό m/f/n	aft-os/i/o	this
αφίξεις, οι	afiksis	arrivals
αφορολόγητος/η/ο m/f/n	aforoloyeet-os/i/o	tax free
αφυδατώνομαι	afeethatonome	to dehydrate

B

βάζω	*vazo*	to put
βάζω μπρος	*vazo mbros*	to start (car)
βαλίτσα, η	*valeetsa*	suitcase
βγάζω ακτινογραφία	*vghazo akteenoghrafeea*	to x-ray
βιασμός, ο	*veeasmos*	rape
βιβλίο, το	*vivlio*	book
βιβλιοθήκη, η	*veevleeotheekee*	library
βίζα, η	*veesa*	visa
βιταμίνη, η	*veetameenee*	vitamin
βλέπω	*vlepo*	to watch
βοήθεια!	*voithia!*	help!
βοηθώ	*voitho*	to help
βορράς, ο	*voras*	north
βροχή, η	*vrokhee*	rain
βρώμικος/η/ο *m/f/n*	*vromeek-os/i/o*	dirty

Γ

γεμίστε το	***yemeeste to***	**fill her up (petrol)**

At a full-service station, round up the bill slightly to reward a helpful attendant.

γήπεδο του γκολφ, το	*yeepedho too golf*	golf course
γήπεδο του τένις, το	*yeepedho too tenees*	tennis court
για	*ya*	for
για μια νύχτα	*yia meea neechta*	overnight
γιατί;	*yiati?*	why?
γιατρός, ο/η *m/f*	*yiatros, o/i*	doctor
γιος, ο	*yios*	son
γιοτ, το	*yacht*	yacht
γκάζι, το	*gazee*	gas
γκαράζ, το	*garaz*	garage
γκολφ, το	*golf*	golf
γλώσσα, η	*ghlosa*	language
γνωρίζω	*gnoreezo*	to know (person)
γονείς, οι	*ghonees*	parents
γράμμα	*ghramma*	letter
γραμματόσημο, το	*ghramatoseemo*	stamp
γραφείο έκδοσης εισητηρίων, το	*grafeeo ekdosis eeseeteereeon*	ticket office
γραφείο, το	*ghrafeeo*	office
γράφω	*ghrafo*	to write
γρήγορα	*ghreeghora*	fast
γρήγορα	*ghreeghora*	quickly
γρήγορος/η/ο *m/f/n*	*ghreeghor-os/i/o*	quick
γρίπη, η	*ghreepi*	flu
γυαλιά ηλίου, τα	*yalya eeleeoo*	sunglasses
γυαλιά, τα	*yalya*	glasses
γυναίκα, η	*yeeneka*	woman

γύρω	***yiro***	**around**

A similar word – γύρος – refers to the meat hunks that spin inside the oven.

Δ

δασμός, ο	*thasmos*	duty (tax)
δείχνω	*dheekhno*	to show
Δεκέμβριος, ο	*thekemvrios*	December
δελτίο επιβιβάσεως, το	*dhelteeo epivivaseos*	boarding card
δεξιά	*dheksya*	right
δημαρχείο, το	*dheemarkheeo*	town hall
δημόσια μέσα μεταφοράς, τα	*dheemoseea mesa metaforas*	public transport
διάβαση πεζών, η	*theeavasi pezon*	zebra crossing

| διαδίκτυο, το | ***thiathiktio*** | web |

Greece periodically bans online gaming (any game, not just gambling). Ask before you play.

διαβατήριο, το	*thiavatirio*	passport
διαδρομή, η	*deeadromee*	route
διαθέσιμος/η/ο *m/f/n*	*thiathesim-os/i/o*	available
διαθέσιμος/η/ο *m/f/n*	*dheeatheseem-os/i/o*	vacant
διακοπές, οι	*dheeakopes*	holiday, vacation
διακοπή	*dheeakopee*	interruption
διάλογος	*dheealoghos*	dialogue
διαμέρισμα, το	*thiamerizma*	apartment
διαμέσου	*dheeamesoo*	through
διασκεδάζω	*dheeaskedhazo*	to enjoy
διασταύρωση, η	*dheeastavrosee*	junction
διαταράσσω	*thiatarasso*	to disturb
διεθνές, το *n*	*dhiethnes*	international (n)
διεθνής, ο/η *m/f*	*dhiethnees, o/i*	international (m/f)
διευθετώ	*thieftheto*	to arrange
διευθυντής, ο	*thieftheendhees*	manager
δικηγόρος, ο	*dheekighoros*	lawyer
δικό μου	*deeko mu*	my
δικός σου	*deekos su*	your (informal)
δικός σας	*deekos sas*	your (formal)
δίνω	*dheeno*	to give
διόδια, τα	*dheeodheea*	toll
διότι	*thioti*	because
δίπλα	*theepla*	by (beside)
δίπλα σε	*dheepla se*	next to
διπλός/ή/ό *m/f/n*	*thipl-os/i/o*	double
διψάω	*dheepsao*	thirsty
δοκιμαστήριο, το	*dhokimastirio*	fitting room
δουλειά, η	*dhoolya*	business
δουλειά, η	*dhoolya*	work
δουλεύω	*dhoolevo*	to work (person)
δρομολόγιο, το	*dromoloyeeo*	itinerary
δρομολόγιο, το	*dromoloyeeo*	timetable
δρόμος, ο	*dhromos*	road
δρόμος, ο	*dhromos*	street
δρόμος, ο	*dromos*	way (route)
δροσερός/ή/ό *m/f/n*	*dhroser-os/i/o*	cool
δυσάρεστος/η/ο *m/f/n*	*deesarest-os/i/o*	unpleasant
δύση, η	*dheesee*	west
δύσκολος/η/ο *m/f/n*	*dheeskol-os/i/o*	difficult

δωμάτιο, το	*thomatio*	room

Travellers on a tight budget often rent rooms in family homes, especially on the islands.

δωρεάν, ο/η/το *m/f/n*	*dhorean, o/ee/to*	free (money)

E

εβδομάδα, η	*evthomatha*	week
εγγύηση, η	*engeeyeesee*	guarantee
εγκαταστάσεις, οι	*eghatastasees*	facilities
έγκλημα, το	*engkleema*	crime
έγκυρος/η/ο *m/f/n*	*engkeer-os/i/o*	valid
εδώ	*etho*	here

είδη καλλωπισμού, τα	*eedi kalopeesmoo*	toiletries

If the airline loses your bag on the outbound trip, ask for a toiletries-and-essentials allowance.

ειδήσεις	*eedheesees*	news
είδος	*eedhos*	kind (sort)
είμαι	*ime*	to be
είναι χαλασμένο	*ine khalasmeno*	off (food)
εισάγω	*isagho*	to import
εισιτήριο, το	*eeseeteereeo*	ticket (bus)
εισιτήριο, το	*eeseeteereeo*	ticket (cinema)
είσοδος, η	*eesodhos*	way in
εκεί	*ekee*	there
εκείνος/η/ο *m/f/n*	*ekeen-os/i/o*	that
έκθεση, η	*ekthesee*	exhibition
έκπτωση, η	*ekptosee*	discount
έκπτωση, η	*ekptosee*	reduction
εκτός λειτουργίας	*ektos leetoorgheeas*	out of order
ελάχιστος/η/ο *m/f/n*	*elakheest-os/i/o*	minimum
ελεύθερος/η/ο *m/f/n*	*eleftheros/i/o*	free (vacant)
έλκος, το	*elkos*	ulcer
Ελλάδα	*eladha*	Greece
Έλληνας/Ελληνίδα *noun m/f*	*elinas/elinidha*	Greek (person)
ελληνικά *(language)*	*elinika*	Greek (language)
ελληνικός/ή/ό *adj m/f/n*	*elinikos/i/o*	Greek (thing)
εμβολιασμός, ο	*emvoleeasmos*	vaccination
εμπορικό κέντρο, το	*emporiko kendro*	shopping centre
ένας άλλος/μία άλλη/ένα άλλο *m/f/n*	*enas alos/mia alee/ena alo*	another
ένας/μία/ένα *m/f/n*	*enas/mia/ena*	a(n)
ενδιαφέρον, το *n*	*endheeaferon*	interesting (n)
ενδιαφέρουσα, η *f*	*endheeaferusa*	interesting (f)
ενδιαφέρων, ο *m*	*endheeaferon*	interesting (m)
εντάξει	*endahksee*	all right/ok
εντολή	*endolee*	order (postal)
έντυπο, το	*enteepo*	form (document)
ενώ	*eno*	while
εξάγω	*eksagho*	to export
έξοδος, η	*eksodhos*	way out

εξοχή, η	*eksokhi*	countryside

On May Day, Greeks tour the countryside with wreaths adorning their car bonnets.

εξυπηρέτηση, η	*ekseepeereteesee*	service
έξω	*ekso*	outside
εξωτερικός χώρος	*eksotereekos horos*	outdoor
επάνω	*epano*	up
επάνω	*epano*	upstairs
επείγον	*epeeghon*	urgent
επείγοντα, τα	*epeeghonda*	A&E
επείγουσα ανάγκη, η	*epeeghusa anaghi*	emergency
επέτειος, η	*epetios*	anniversary
επιβεβαιώνω	*epeeveveono*	to confirm
επιβεβαίωση, η	*epeeveveosi*	confirmation
επικοινωνώ με	*epeekeenono me*	to contact
επίσης	*epeesees*	too
επισκέπτομαι	*epeeskeptomai*	to visit
επίσκεψη, η	*epeeskepsee*	visit
επιστροφή χρημάτων, η	*epeestrofee khrimaton*	refund
επιταγή, η	*epitayee*	cheque
επόμενος/η/ο *m/f/n*	*epomen-os/i/o*	next
επώνυμο, το	*eponeemo*	surname
ερείπια, τα	*ereepya*	ruins

ερώτηση, η	*eroteesee*	question

Greeks' 'friendly' questions can feel more like interrogations at times. Respect their culture – and your limits too.

εσείς	*esees*	you (formal)
εσύ	*esee*	you (informal)
εσώρουχα, τα	*esorookha*	underwear
ετήσιος/α/ο *m/f/n*	*eteesi-os/a/o*	yearly
ετικέτα, η	*eteeketa*	label
έτοιμος/η/ο *m/f/n*	*eteem-os/i/o*	ready
ευγενικός/ή/ό *m/f/n*	*efgheneek-os/i/o*	kind (nice)
ευθεία, η	*eftheea*	straight
εφημερίδα, η	*efeemereedha*	newspaper
εχθές	*ekthes*	yesterday
έχω	*ekho*	to have
έχω δίκιο	*eho deekyo*	to be right

Z

ζέστη, η	*zestee*	heat
ζεστός/ή/ό *m/f/n*	*zest-os/i/o*	hot
ζευγάρι, το	*zevgharee*	pair
ζημιά, η	*zimia*	damage
ζητάω	*zeetao*	to request
ζώνη ασφαλείας, η	*zoni asfalias*	seat belt
ζώνη, η	*zonee*	zone
ζωολογικός κήπος, ο	*zo-oloyeekos keepos*	zoo

Η

ή	*ee*	or
ήλιος, ο	*eelios*	sun

ημέιλ/e-mail, το	*imeil*	e-mail
ημέρα, η	*imera*	day
ημερομηνία, η	*imeromin<u>ee</u>a*	date (calendar)
ηρεμιστικό, το	*eeremist<u>ee</u>ko*	sedative
ήσυχος/η/ο *m/f/n*	*isikh-<u>os</u>/i/o*	quiet

Θ

θάλασσα, η	*th<u>a</u>lasa*	sea
θαλάσσια σπορ, τα	*thal<u>a</u>seea spor*	water sports
θαυμάσιος/α/ο *m/f/n*	*thav<u>ma</u>see-os/a/o*	wonderful
θέλω	*th<u>e</u>lo*	to want
θέση, η	*th<u>e</u>see*	seat

Ι

Ιανουάριος, ο	*ianu<u>a</u>rios*	January
ιδιοκτήτης, ο *m*	*eedheeokt<u>ee</u>tees*	owner (m)
ιδιοκτήτρια, η *f*	*eedheeokt<u>ee</u>tria*	owner (f)
ιδιωτικός/ή/ό *m/f/n*	*eedheeoteek-<u>os</u>/i/o*	private

Ιούλιος, ο	***iulios***	**July**

In summer, Athenians flee the **meltemi**, the hot winds that scour the Saronic Gulf.

Ιούνιος, ο	*iunios*	June
ιππασία, η	*ipasia*	horse riding
ιππεύω	*eepevo*	to ride (horse)
Ιρλανδία, η	*eerlandh<u>ee</u>a*	Ireland
ιρλανδικά *(language)*	*eerlandeeka*	Irish (language)
ιρλανδικός/ή/ό *adj m/f/n*	*eerlandikos/i/o*	Irish (thing)
Ιρλανδός/Ιρλανδή *noun m/f*	*eerlandh<u>os</u>/ eerlandh<u>ee</u>*	Irish (person)
ιστοσελίδα, η	*eestosel<u>ee</u>da*	website

ίσως	***<u>ee</u>sos***	**maybe**

'Maybe' often means 'no', much like in Arab countries (the Ottomans, after all, ruled Greece for centuries).

ίσως	*<u>ee</u>sos*	perhaps

Κ

καζίνο, το	*kaz<u>ee</u>no*	casino
καθαριστήριο, το	*kathareest<u>ee</u>reeo*	dry-cleaner's
καθημερινή, η	*katheemeren<u>ee</u>*	weekday
καθόλου	*kath<u>o</u>lu*	any
καθυστερημένος/η/ο *m/f/n*	*katheesterimen-os/i/o*	late (delayed)
καθυστέρηση, η	*katheest<u>e</u>risi*	delay
και	*ke*	and
καινούριος/α/ο *m/f/n*	*ken<u>oo</u>ry-os/a/o*	new
καιρός, ο	*ker<u>os</u>*	weather
καίω	*k<u>e</u>o*	to burn
καλός/ή/ό *m/f/n*	*kal-<u>os</u>/i/o*	good
καλός/ή/ό *m/f/n*	*kal-<u>os</u>/i/o*	nice (people)
καλύτερος/η/ο *m/f/n*	*kal<u>i</u>ter-os/i/o*	better
καλώς ήλθατε	*kal<u>o</u>s eelthate*	welcome
κάνε γρήγορα!	*k<u>a</u>ne ghr<u>i</u>ghora!*	hurry up!

κάνω!	kano	to make
κάνω εμετό	kano emeto	to vomit
κάνω κράτηση	kano kratisi	to book
κάνω κράτηση	kano kratisi	to reserve
κάνω λάθος	kano lathos	wrong (mistaken)
κάνω ποδήλατο	kano podheelato	to ride (bicycle)

καπνίζω	**kapneezo**	**to smoke**

Europe's heaviest smoking nation is trying to cut back,
banning cigarettes from many public places.

καπνός, ο	kapnos	tobacco
κατά τη διάρκεια	kata tee dheearkeea	during
καταλαβαίνω	katalaveno	to understand
κατάλυμα, το	katalima	accommodation
καταλύω (σε ξενοδοχείο)	kataleeo (se ksenothoheeo)	to check in (hotel)
κατεπείγον, το	katepeeghon	express (delivery)
κάτι	katee	something
κάτω	kato	down
κάτω από	kato apo	under
καφετερία, η	kafeteria	café
κέντρο, το	kentro	centre
κινηματογράφος, ο	keeneematoghrafos	cinema
κινητό τηλέφωνο, το	keeneeto tilefono	mobile phone
κλαμπ, το	klab	club
κλειδί, το	kleedhee	key
κλείνω	kleeno	to close
κλειστός/ή/ό m/f/n	kleest-os/i/o	closed
κλειστός/ή/ό m/f/n	kleest-os/i/o	shut
κλήση, η	kleesee	ticket (parking)
κλοπή, η	klopee	theft
κόβω	kovo	to cut
κοιμάμαι	keemame	to sleep
κοιτάζω	keetazo	to look
κομμωτήριο, το	komoteerio	hairdresser's
κομπιουτεράκι, το	kombiuteraki	calculator
κοντά	konda	near
κοντινός/ή/ό m/f/n	kondeen-os/i/o	close by
κοντός/ή/ό m/f/n	kond-os/i/o	short
κόρη, η	kori	daughter
κορίτσι, το	koreetsee	girl
κόσμος, ο	kosmos	world
κοστίζει	kosteezee	to cost
κόστος, το	kostos	cost (the)
κουίζ, το	quiz	quiz
κουνούπι, το	koonoopee	mosquito
κουρασμένος/η/ο m/f/n	koorasmen-os/i/o	tired
κόψιμο, το	kopseemo	cut
κράτηση, η	kratisi	booking
κράτηση, η	kratisi	reservation
κρατώ	krato	to keep
κρέμα, η	krema	cream
κρύος/α/ο m/f/n	kree-os/a/o	cold
κτυπώ	kteepo	to knock

κυρία, η	keereea	lady
κυρία, η	keereea	madam
κύριος, ο	kirios	sir
κυρίως	keereeos	main

Λ

λάθος, το	lathos	error
λαμβάνω	lamvano	to receive
λείπει	leepee	missing
λειτουργεί	leetooryee	to work (machine)
λέξη, η	leksee	word
λεξικό χρήσιμων φράσεων, το	leksiko chrisimon fraseon	phrase book
λεπτό, το	lepto	minute
λεωφορείο, το	leoforio	bus
ληστεύω	leestevo	to rob
λίγο	leegho	little (a little)
λιγότερος/η/ο m/f/n	leeghoter-os/i/o	less
λιμάνι, το	leemanee	port (sea)
λογαριασμός, ο	loghariazmos	bill

Μ

Μάιος, ο	ma-ee-os	May
μακριά	makreea	away
μακριά	makreea	far
μαλακός/ή/ό m/f/n	malak-os/i/o	soft
μαλλιά, τα	malya	hair
Μάρτιος, ο	martios	March
με	me	by
με	me	with
μεγάλος/η/ο m/f/n	meghal-os/i/o	big
μερικοί/ές/ά m/f/n	mereekee/es/a	some
μέσα	mesa	in

| **μεσάνυχτα, τα** | **mesaneekhta** | **midnight** |

Greeks party late into the night, often heading to clubs at midnight.

μεσημέρι, το	mesimeri	midday
μεταδοτικός/ή/ό m/f/n	metathotik-os/i/o	contagious
μεταφράζω	metafrazo	to translate
μετρητά, τα	metrita	cash
μετρό, το	metro	underground (tube)
μηδέν, το	mithen	zero
μήνυμα, το	meeneema	message
μητέρα, η	meetera	mother
μητρόπολη, η	mitropoli	cathedral
μηχάνημα ανάληψης χρημάτων (ATM), το	mihanima analipsis chrimaton (ey tee em)	cashpoint
μηχανικός, ο	meekhaneekos	mechanic
μία φορά	meea fora	once
μικρός/ή/ό m/f/n	meekr-os/i/o	small
μιούζικαλ, το	miuzeekal	musical
μισό, το	meeso	half
μόνο	mono	just (only)

μόνο	_mono_	only
μου αρέσει	moo a_res_ee	to like
μου λείπει	moo _lee_pee	to miss (a person)
μουσείο, το	moo_seeo_	museum
μπάνιο, το	_banio_	bath
μπαρ, το	bar	bar (pub)
μπίζνες κλας, η	_biznes_ klas	business class
μπορώ	boro	can (to be able)
μπρελόκ, το	brel_ok_	keyring
μωρό, το	mor_o_	baby

N

ναι	ne	yes
ναρκωτικό, το	narkotee_ko_	drug
ναυαγοσώστης, ο	navagho_sos_tees	lifeguard
νέος/α/ο m/f/n	_ne_-os/a/o	young
νερό, το	ne_ro_	water
νησί, το	nees_ee_	island
νικώ	nee_ko_	to win
Νοέμβριος, ο	no_em_vrios	November
νοίκι, το	_nee_kee	rent
νοικιάζω	nee_kia_zo	to hire
νόμισμα, το	_no_misma	currency
νοσοκομείο, το	nosoko_mio_	hospital
νοτιοαφρικανικός/ή/ό adj m/f/n	noteeoafrikani_kos_/i/o	South African (thing)
Νοτιοαφρικάνος/α noun m/f	noteeoafri_ka_nos/a	South African (person)
Νότιος Αφρική, η	_no_teeos afri_ki_	South Africa
νότος, ο	_no_tos	south
ντισκοτέκ, η	deesko_tek_	disco
νύχτα, η	_nee_khta	night
νυχτερινό κέντρο, το	neekhteree_no_ _ken_dro	nightclub
νωρίς	nor_ees_	early

Ξ

ξαφνικά	ksafnee_ka_	suddenly
ξεκουράζομαι	ksekoo_ra_zome	to relax
ξεναγός, το	ksenag_hos_	guide
ξένο συνάλλαγμα, το	_kse_no sina_lagh_ma	bureau de change
ξενοφοβία	ksenofo_vee_a	xenophobia
ξενόφοβος/η/ο m/f/n	kse_no_fov-os/i/o	xenophobe
ξενώνας νεότητας, ο	kse_no_nas neo_tee_tas	youth hostel
ξέρω	_kse_ro	to know (knowledge)
ξυπνητήρι, το	ksipni_ti_ri	alarm
ξυραφάκι, το	kseera_fa_kee	razor blade

O

ο καλύτερος/η καλύτερη/το καλύτερο m/f/n	o ka_li_teros/i ka_li_teri/to ka_li_tero	best
ο περισσότερος/η περισσότερη/το περισσότερο m/f/n	o peree_so_teros/i peree_so_teri/to peree_so_tero	most
οδηγίες, οι	odhigh_ee_-es	directions

οδηγός, ο/η	odhighos, o/i	driver
οδηγώ	odhigho	to drive
Οκτώβριος, ο	oktovrios	October
όλοι	oli	all
ομάδα, η	omadha	group
όμορφος/η/ο m/f/n	omorf-os/i/o	pretty

| ομοφυλόφιλος/η/ο m/f/n | omofeelofil-os/i/o | homosexual |

Athens and cosmopolitan islands like Mykonos welcome gays, but rural areas may require some discretion.

ομπρέλα, η	ombrela	umbrella
όνομα, το	onoma	name
οξυγόνο, το	okseeghono	oxygen
οπτικός, ο/η m/f	optikos, o/i	optician's
οργανισμός τουρισμού, ο	orghaneesmos toorismoo	tourist office
Ουαλία, η	ooaleea	Wales
ουαλικά (language)	ooalika	Welsh (language)
ουαλικός/ή/ό adj m/f/n	ooalik-os/i/o	Welsh (thing)
Ουαλός/ή noun m/f	ooalos/i	Welsh (person)
ουρά, η	oora	queue
όχημα, το	okheema	vehicle

Π

παιδί, το	pedhee	kid
παιδιά, τα	pethia	children
παιδικό κρεβάτι, το	pethiko krevati	cot
παίρνω	perno	to get
παίρνω	perno	to take
πακέτο, το	paketo	carton (cigarettes)
πάλι	pali	again
παμπ, η	pab	pub
παντρεμένος/η/ο m/f/n	padremen-os/i/o	married
πάνω	pano	on
πάρα	para	very
παραγγέλλω	parangelo	to order
παραδίδω τις αποσκευές μου και παίρνω κάρτα επιβίβασης	paratheetho tis aposkeves mu ke perno karta epivivasis	to check in (airport)
παραλία, η	paralia	beach

| παραλία γυμνιστών, η | paraleea yeemneeston | nudist beach |

Going topless is acceptable on most beaches, but only strip bare in designated zones.

παράπονο, το	parapono	complaint
παραπονούμαι	paraponoome	to complain
παράσταση, η	parastasee	show (a)
παρκάρω	parkaro	to park
πάρκο, το	parko	park
πάρτυ, το	party	party
πατέρας, ο	pateras	father
παυσίπονο, το	pafseepono	painkiller

πεινώ	peeno	to be hungry
πελάτης, ο	pelatees	customer
περιοχή, η	periohi	area
περίπτερο, το	pereeptero	kiosk
περισσότερο	pereesotero	more
περπατώ	perpato	to walk
πηγαίνω	peeyeno	to go
πιάτσα ταξί, η	pyatsa taksee	taxi rank
πιθανό	peethano	possible
πιθανώς	peethanos	probably
πινακίδα, η	peenakeedha	sign
πινακοθήκη, η	peenakotheekee	gallery
πισίνα, η	pisina	swimming pool
πιστωτική κάρτα, η	pistotiki karta	credit card
πίσω	piso	back (place)
πλένω	pleno	to wash
πληκτρολόγιο, το	pleektrologhio	keyboard
πληροφορίες, οι	pliroforee-es	information
πληρώνω	plirono	to pay
πλούσιος/α/ο m/f/n	ploosee-os/a/o	rich
πλυντήριο, το	pleendeereeo	launderette
ποδηλασία, η	podheelasia	cycling
ποδήλατο, το	pothilato	bicycle
ποδόσφαιρο, το	podhosfero	football
ποιο;	pio?	which?
ποιος;	pios?	who?
ποιότητα, η	peeoteeta	quality
πόλη, η	polee	city
πόλη, η	polee	town
πολλοί/ές/ά m/f/n	polee/es/a	many
πολύ	polee	much
πολύτιμα αντικείμενα, τα	poleeteema andeekeemena	valuables
πονώ	pono	to hurt
πορτό, το	porto	port (drink)

| **πορτοφόλι, το** | ***portofolee*** | **wallet** |

Don't insult a host's generosity: generally, whoever invites pays the bill.

πόση ώρα;	posee ora?	how long? (time)
πόσο κοστίζει;	poso kosteezee?	how much? (money)
πόσο μακριά;	poso makreea?	how far?
πόσο μεγάλος/η/ο; m/f/n	poso meghalos/i/o?	how big?
ποσότητα, η	posoteeta	quantity
ποτέ	pote	never
πότε;	pote?	when?
πού;	pu?	where?
πουθενά	puthena	nowhere
πουλώ	poolo	to sell
πούρο, το	pooro	cigar
πράγμα, το	praghma	thing
πραγματικός/ή/ό m/f/n	praghmateek-os/i/o	real
πρατήριο βενζίνης, το	pratirio venzeenis	filling (station)
πρέπει	prepee	must

πρεσβεία, η	presveea	embassy
πριν	prin	ago
πρόβλημα, το	provlima	problem
προξενείο, το	prokseneeo	consulate
προσωπικό, το	prosopiko	staff
προτιμώ	proteemo	to prefer
πρώτες βοήθειες, οι	protes voeetheeyes	first aid
πτήση, η	ptisi	flight
πώς;	pos?	how?

Ρ

ραδιόφωνο, το	radheeofono	radio
ραντεβού, το	radevu	appointment
ρολόι, το	roloee	watch (the)
ρούχα, τα	rookha	clothes
ρωτάω	rotao	to ask
ρωτώ	roto	to query

Σ

Σαββατοκύριακο, το	savatokiriako	weekend
σάουνα, η	sauna	sauna
σβηστός/ή/ό m/f/n	sveest-os/i/o	off (switched)
σε	se	at
σε	se	to
σελφ σέρβις, το	self service	self-service
Σεπτέμβριος, ο	septemvrios	September
σερβίρω	serveero	to serve
σερβιτόρα, η	serveetora	waitress
σερβιτόρος, ο	serveetoros	waiter
σήμερα	seemera	today
σιδηρόδρομος, ο	seedheerodhromos	railway
σκέφτομαι	skeftomai	to think
σκι, το	ski	ski
σκοτώνω	skotono	to kill
σκούφος μπάνιου, ο	skoofos baniu	bathing cap
Σκωτία, η	skoteea	Scotland
σκωτσέζικος/η/ο adj m/f/n	skotsezikos/i/o	Scottish (thing)
Σκωτσέζος/α noun m/f	skotsezos/a	Scottish (person)
σπορ, το	spor	sport
σπουδαίος/α/ο m/f/n	spoodh-eos/a/o	important
στάδιο, το	stadheeo	stadium
στάθμευση, η	stathmefsi	parking
σταθμός, ο	stathmos	station
σταματώ	stamato	to stop
στεγνοκαθαρίζω	steghnokathareezo	to dry clean
στέλνω	stelno	to send
στέλνω sms	stelno sms	to text
στέλνω φαξ	stelno faks	to fax
στιγμή, η	steegmee	moment
στο εσωτερικό	sto esotereeko	inside
συγχαρητήρια!	seenkhareeteereea!	congratulations!
σύζυγος, η	sizighos	wife
σύζυγος, ο	sizighos	husband
συλλαβίζω	seelaveezo	to spell
σύμπτωμα, το	seemptoma	symptom

συνάντηση, η	*seenandisi*	meeting
συναντώ	*seenando*	to meet
συνήθως	*seeneethos*	usually

συνταγή, η	*seendayee*	prescription
συνταξιούχος, ο/η *m/f*	*seendakseeookhos, o/i*	retired
σύντομα	*seendoma*	soon
σχετικά με	*shetika me*	about (concerning)
σωσίβιο, το	*soseeveeo*	life jacket

T

τουαλέτα, η	*tooaleta*	toilet
τα λέμε αργότερα	*ta leme arghotera*	see you later
ταινία, η	*teneea*	film (cinema)
ταμείο, το	*tamio*	box office
ταμπόν, το	*tambon*	tampons
ταξί, το	*taksi*	taxi
ταξιδεύω	*takseedhevo*	travel
ταξίδι, το	*takseedhee*	journey
ταξιδιωτικό πρακτορείο, το	*takseedhyoteeko praktoreeo*	travel agency
ταράτσα, η	*taratsa*	terrace
ταυτότητα, η	*taftoteeta*	identity card
ταχεία, η	*takheea*	express (train)
ταχυδρομείο, το	*takheedhromeeo*	mail
ταχυδρομείο, το	*takheedhromeeo*	post office
ταχυδρομικός κωδικός, ο	*tahithromikos kothikos*	area code
ταχυδρομώ	*takheedhromo*	post
ταχύτητα, η	*takheeteeta*	speed
τελειώνω	*teleeono*	to finish
τελευταίος/α/ο *m/f/n*	*telefte-os/a/o*	last
τελωνείο, το	*teloneeo*	customs
τένις, το	*tenees*	tennis
τέταρτο, το	*tetarto*	quarter
τέχνη, η	*tehni*	art
τζετ σκι, το	*jetski*	jet ski
τηλεόραση, η	*teeleorasee*	television
τηλεφων-ητής/ήτρια *m/f*	*tilefon-itis/itria*	operator
τηλεφωνικός θάλαμος, ο	*teelefoneekos thalamos*	telephone box
τηλέφωνο, το	*tilefono*	phone
τηλέφωνο, το	*tilefono*	telephone
τηλεφωνώ	*tilefono*	to call
τηλεφωνώ	*tilefono*	to dial
τηλεφωνώ	*tilefono*	to phone
τηλεφωνώ	*tilefono*	to ring (a person)
τι μήκος έχει;	*tee meekos echee?*	how long? (length)
τι;	*tee?*	what?
τιμή συναλλάγματος, η	*timi seenalaghmatos*	exchange rate
τιμή, η	*teemi*	charge

τιμή, η	*teemi*	price
τίποτα	*teepota*	nothing
τοπικός/ή/ό *m/f/n*	*topeek-os/i/o*	local
τόπος, ο	*topos*	place
τότε	*tote*	then
τουαλέτα ανδρών, η	*tualeta andhron*	gents
τουαλέτα γυναικών, η	*tualeta yeenekon*	ladies (toilets)

| τραμ, το | *tram* | tram |

The tram between Athens and its port, Piraeus, is not air-conditioned. Dress lightly in summer or suffer.

τραπεζαρία, η	*trapezareea*	dining room
τραπέζι, το	*trapezee*	table
τρένο, το	*treno*	train
τρέχω	*trekho*	to run
τρόπος, ο	*tropos*	way (manner)
τροφική δηλητηρίαση, η	*trofeeki dhilitireeasee*	food poisoning
τρώω	*tro-o*	to eat
τσιγάρο, το	*tseegharo*	cigarette
τσούχτρα, η	*tsookhtra*	jellyfish
τυπικός/ή/ό *m/f/n*	*teepeek-os/i/o*	typical
τώρα	*tora*	now

Υ

υγιές *n*	*eeyee-es*	well (healthy)
υγιής *m/f*	*eeyee-ees*	well (healthy)
υπάλληλος υποδοχής, ο/η *m/f*	*ipalilos ipothokhis, o/i*	receptionist
υπηκοότητα, η	*epeeko-oteeta*	nationality
υπνωτικό χάπι, το	*eepnoteeko khapee*	sleeping pill
υπογραφή, η	*eepoghrafee*	signature
υπογράφω	*eepoghrafo*	to sign
υποδοχή, η	*ipothokhi*	reception

Φ

Φεβρουάριος, ο	*fevruarios*	February
φερμουάρ, το	*fermooar*	zip
φεύγω	*fevgho*	to leave
φίλη, η *f*	*fili*	friend (female)
φιλί, το	*feeli*	kiss
φιλμ, το	*feelm*	film (camera)
φιλοδώρημα, το	*filodhoreema*	tip (money)
φίλος, ο *m*	*filos*	friend (male)
φιλώ	*feelo*	to kiss
φόρος, ο	*foros*	tax
ΦΠΑ, ο	*fee pee a*	VAT
φρόνιμος/η/ο *m/f/n*	*fronim-os/i/o*	sensible
φτηνός/ή/ό *m/f/n*	*fteen-os/i/o*	cheap
φωτιά, η	*fotya*	fire
φωτογραφία, η	*fotoghrafeea*	photo
φωτογραφική μηχανή, η	*fotoghrafiki meekhani*	camera

X

χάνω	*khano*	to lose
χάνω	*khano*	to miss (a train)
χάρτης δρόμου, ο	*khartees dhromoo*	map (road)
χάρτης πόλης, ο	*khartees polis*	map (city)
χαρτονόμισμα, το	*khartonomeesma*	note (money)
χειρότερος/η/ο *m/f/n*	*kheeroter-os/i/o*	worse

χορτοφάγος, ο/η   **_khortofaghos, o/i_**   **vegetarian**
Rural restaurants sometimes run out of vegetarian standards, favourites with the omnivores, too. Order early.

χρειάζομαι	*khriazome*	to need
χρεώνω	*khreono*	to charge
χρήματα, τα	*khrimata*	money
χρηματοκιβώτιο, το	*khrimatokivotio*	safe
χρησιμοποιώ	*khreeseemopyo*	to use
χρήσιμος/η/ο *m/f/n*	*khreeseem-os/i/o*	useful
χρόνος, ο	*khronos*	time
χρόνος, ο	*khronos*	year
Χρυσός Οδηγός, ο	*chreesos odheeghos*	yellow pages
χρώμα, το	*khroma*	colour
χώρα, η	*khora*	country
χωρίς	*khorees*	without

ψ

ψηλός/ή/ό *m/f/n*	*pseel-os/i/o*	high
ψηλός/ή/ό *m/f/n*	*pseel-os/i/o*	tall
ψώνια, τα	*psonia*	shopping
ψωνίζω	*psoneezo*	to shop

Ω

| ώρα, η | *ora* | time (clock) |
| ωραίος/α/ο *m/f/n* | *ore-os/a/o* | nice (things) |

Quick reference

Numbers

0	μηδέν	*meethen*
1	ένας/μία/ένα *m/f/n*	*enas/mia/ena*
2	δύο	*thio*
3	τρεις/τρία *m&f/n*	*trees/treea*
4	τέσσερις/τέσσερα *m&f/n*	*teseris/tesera*
5	πέντε	*pende*
6	έξι	*eksi*
7	εφτά	*efta*
8	οχτώ	*okhto*
9	εννέα	*enea*
10	δέκα	*theka*
11	έντεκα	*endeka*
12	δώδεκα	*thotheka*
13	δεκατρείς/δεκατρία *m&f/n*	*thekatris/thekatria*
14	δεκατέσσερις/ δεκατέσσερα *m&f/n*	*thekateseris/ thekatesera*
15	δεκαπέντε	*thekapende*
16	δεκαέξι	*thekaeksi*
17	δεκαεφτά	*thekaefta*
18	δεκαοχτώ	*thekaokhto*
19	δεκαεννέα	*thekaenea*
20	είκοσι	*Ikosi*
21	είκοσι ένας/μία/ένα *m/f/n*	*ikosi enas/mia/ena*
30	τριάντα	*trianda*
40	σαράντα	*saranda*
50	πενήντα	*peninda*
60	εξήντα	*eksinda*
70	εβδομήντα	*evthominda*
80	ογδόντα	*oghthonda*
90	ενενήντα	*eneninda*
100	εκατό	*ekato*
1000	χίλια	*hilia*
1st	πρώτος/πρώτη/πρώτο *m/f/n*	*protos/proti/proto*
2nd	δεύτερος/δεύτερη/δεύτερο *m/f/n*	*thefteros/thefteri/ theftero*
3rd	τρίτος/τρίτη/τρίτο *m/f/n*	*tritos/triti/trito*
4th	τέταρτος/τέταρτη/τέταρτο *m/f/n*	*tetartos/tetarti/tetarto*
5th	πέμπτος/πέμπτη/πέμπτο *m/f/n*	*pemtos/pemti/pemto*

Weights & measures

gram (=0.03oz)	γραμμάριο	*ghramario*
kilogram (=2.2lb)	κιλό	*kilo*
centimetre (=0.4in)	εκατοστό	*ekatosto*
metre (=1.1yd)	μέτρο	*metro*
kilometre (=0.6m)	χιλιόμετρο	*hiliometro*
litre (=2.1pt)	λίτρο	*litro*

Days & time

Monday	Δευτέρα	*theftera*
Tuesday	Τρίτη	*triti*
Wednesday	Τετάρτη	*tetarti*
Thursday	Πέμπτη	*pemti*
Friday	Παρασκευή	*paraskevi*
Saturday	Σάββατο	*savato*
Sunday	Κυριακή	*kiriaki*
What time is it?	Τι ώρα είναι;	*ti ora ine?*
(Four) o'clock	(Τέσσερις) η ώρα	*(teseris) i ora*
Quarter past (six)	(Έξι) και τέταρτο	*(eksi) ke tetarto*
Half past (eight)	(Οχτώ) και μισή	*(okhto) ke misi*
Quarter to (ten)	(Δέκα) παρά τέταρτο	*(theka) para tetarto*
morning	πρωί	*proi*
afternoon	απόγευμα	*apoyevma*
evening	βράδυ	*vrathi*
night	νύχτα	*nikhta*

Clothes size conversions

Women's clothes	34	36	38	40	42	44	46	50
equiv. UK size	6	8	10	12	14	16	18	20
Men's jackets	44	46	48	50	52	54	56	58
equiv. UK size	34	36	38	40	42	44	46	48
Men's shirts	36	37	38	39	40	41	42	43
equiv. UK size	14	14.5	15	15.5	16	16.5	17	17.5
Shoes	36/37	37/38	39	40	41/42	42/43	44	45
equiv. UK size	4	5	6	7	8	9	10	11